Countering Bullying

Initiatives by schools and local authorities

Delwyn Tattum and Graham Herbert

Trentham Books

First published in 1993 by Trentham Books Limited

Trentham Books Limited
Westview House
734 London Road
Oakhill
Stoke-on-Trent
Staffordshire
England ST4 5NP

British Library Cataloguing Publication Data
A catalogue record for this book is available from the British
Library.

ISBN: 0 948080 85 X

Designed and typeset by Trentham Print Design Limited
and printed in Great Britain by BPCC Wheatons Limited, Exeter.

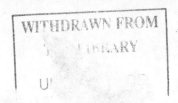

Countering Bullying

'005

}

Contents

Foreword   vii

Preface   ix

Acknowledgements   xiii

Introducing the project   1
Delwyn Tattum

Theme One: Management Strategies   15

   Glapton Primary School, Nottingham   17

   Shirehampton Infant School, Avon   29

   Exwick Middle School, Exeter   36

   Wycliffe College, Stonehouse, Gloucestershire   41

   Eastbourne Comprehensive School, Darlington   48

   St. Mary's C. of E. Primary School, Manchester   52

Theme Two: Using the Curriculum   61

   St John Wall R.C. Comprehensive School, Birmingham   63

   Malvern Girls' College   69

   Pensby High School for Boys, Wirral   76

   Editor's Commentary   80

Theme Three: Transition   85

Lakeside Primary School, Cardiff   87

South Craven High School, West Yorkshire   96

Minsthorpe High School and Community College, West Yorkshire 104

Millfield School, Street, Somerset   113

Theme Four: Educational and Other Agencies   123

Beaumont Leys School, Leicester   125

Cardinal Newman R.C. School, Luton   139

Woodside Junior School, Waltham Forest   146

The Ulster Quaker Peace Education Project   151

Theme Five: Local Education Authorities   161

Gwynedd Education Authority   163

Lothian Regional Council   173

Reflections and Perceptions   179
Graham Herbert

References   191

Author Index   193

Subject Index   195

Foreword

In recent years the Gulbenkian Foundation's Education programme has sought to address the problem of bullying in schools. Our starting point was to try and raise awareness of the prevalence of bullying, as well as its damaging effects on children, and to convey to schools that specific measures could be adopted to reduce it. To this end we funded the publication of a range of advisory materials for teachers, governors and parents. Of these, a practical booklet for schools entitled *Bullying: A Positive Response* proved especially popular and, in due course, influential. Schools that had purchased copies were soon motivated to develop their own positive responses to bullying. It was at this point that the authors of the booklet, Delwyn Tattum and Graham Herbert, approached the Foundation and asked if we could provide support for a further publication that presented as examples of good practice some of the anti-bullying initiatives that the earlier publication has given rise to. The result is this book. It represents a break with the earlier literature for it does not look ahead to what schools and local authorities might achieve: it looks back on what some of them have achieved already. To that extent it is of its time, as well as a measure of the distance that schools and LEAs have travelled — and inevitably only a proportion are here represented — in developing their own anti-bullying initiatives. May the commitment and enterprise of the projects described in this book encourage others to take up the challenge.

Simon Richey, Assistant Director (Education) Gulbenkian Foundation

Preface

This book fits into the second phase of work into the problem of bullying, as it represents those avant-garde schools who have set up anti bullying initiatives to counter bullying behaviour. It is only in the last 6 years that we in the United Kingdom have taken the problem seriously [see the section on Growing Awareness, page 2]. Initially, the main initiative was to convince members of the teaching profession and general public that bullying is an extensive and serious problem. That part of the work is far from finished, as there continue to be many schools which make the dangerous and self-deceptive claim that they do not have any bullying. Such a misplaced attitude can contribute to the secretive climate that results in the unwillingness of children to tell teachers that they or their friends are being bullied. Their school's position makes them feel ashamed because they are different from the pupil image projected by their school. Similarly, bullies derive encouragement from the school's view of itself, because they are able to continue their cruel and damaging behaviour in the belief that at best teachers will not intervene and at worst they will not condemn their behaviour.

A message of 'non-action' will also be conveyed to parents, who will be discouraged from visiting the school to report a case of bullying. They anticipate an unbelieving and unsupportive response, and maybe they will be accused of being 'over-protective'. In a climate of image-protection teachers are too frequently 'economic with the truth' when discussing matters of indiscipline in their school. What is required of teachers is an open acceptance that bullying takes place in *all* schools — including their own. The sixteen schools which have contributed to this book faced up to the fact that in their school community they have some pupils who bully and some who are bullied. Whenever we bring together large numbers of children there will be some who are more aggressive and abusive than the great majority of pupils. Moreover, there will be some children who are vulnerable, because they cannot cope with harsh physical aggression or verbal abuse of their persons, family or race — their upbringing has not prepared them for such unprovoked assaults. The schools in this book recognised that fact and set about, in their various ways, to protect not only the vulnerable ten percent but also the whole school commun. . which cannot tolerate one member abusing, humiliating or oppressing another. Thus, using the booklet, *Bullying: a Positive Response* [Tattum & Herbert, 1990] as their starting point, they set about devising strategies to reduce the incidence of bullying. They travelled along different tracks which we have reduced to five identifiable themes:

Management Strategies

Using the Curriculum

Transition between schools

Using educational and other agencies

Local authority direction and guidance.

These five themes are not independent but interrelated, and it is for each individual school to select and apply the strategies described in the following pages to their own special needs and circumstances. There are many imaginative ideas described and evaluated, and the contributions have been written by a contact person or persons in each school or local authority. We have teachers writing with enthusiasm and imagination and sharing their ideas with fellow teachers.

It is at this point that I return to my opening sentence in which I describe this book as entering into the second phase of work to reduce bullying. It is second phase because these schools have accepted the fact of bullying and decided to address it head on. In their view, the time for talking has ended and the time for doing has started. And in their modest way they are prepared to go public and share their efforts, in the belief that the time has come for *all* schools to tackle the problem of bullying.

We have contributions from England, Scotland, Wales and Northern Ireland. The schools represent both the state and independent sectors, and single-sex and co-educational schools, and cover the full age range from nursery-infant through to large comprehensives. There are schools which serve rural and urban communities, and those which have differing social, cultural and ethnic catchment areas. In fact, we have tried to represent many educational and social variables, to enable most schools to identify with the problems encountered by at least one of the contributing schools.

Graham and I wish to thank all the contributors named and also the very many teachers and pupils not named, but who gave willingly of their time, energy and creativity. We would most particularly wish to express our appreciation to the headteachers, governors and senior local authority officers, without whose support and encouragement this work would not have been possible. All those involved in the project acknowledge that it is only the beginning of their anti-bullying campaign. Realistically, they know that bullying in schools cannot be eradicated, only reduced and contained, for every day brings new problems and every year a new intake. The great value of these initiatives is that each school has created a climate of caring and support into which new pupils will be initiated by the present pupil body. Their motto may well be 'sharing and caring'.

Finally, we wish to acknowledge the support and encouragement given to use by the Calouste Gulbenkian Foundation. They funded the production of *Bullying: a Positive Response* and assisted us with this latest initiative. As a caring organisation they have worked to raise the issue of bullying in a variety of ways and so helped many unhappy children and their families.

Delwyn Tattum
April, 1993

Acknowledgements

This book was published by Trentham Books in association with the Calouste Gulbenkian Foundation and Cardiff Institute of Higher Education.

Introducing the project

Delwyn Tattum

Conceiving the project

 It would not have been possible to write a book like this as recently as three years ago. Firstly, because the recognition of bullying as a serious problem in our schools has only taken place in the last 4-5 years. The second reason is that teachers, and headteachers in particular, have been most reluctant to raise bullying as an issue for fear of giving the impression to parents and others that they have a violent school. This misplaced caution is a dangerous view for teachers to hold, as it means that at best they are ignoring the problem and at worst they can be accused of tacitly condoning aggressive behaviour by a proportion of pupils. It is to the great credit of the schools which have contributed to this book that they tackled the problem and showed themselves to be pioneers in this field of caring. They thus placed the well-being of their pupils above all other considerations. But it would be wrong to give the impression that these were the only schools in the United Kingdom who had, in those early days, devised policies and programmes to counter bullying. So how were these sixteen schools and other organisations chosen?

The project has its origins in the publication of the booklet *Bullying: A Positive Response* (Tattum & Herbert) in April 1990. The production of this booklet was supported by funds from the Calouste Gulbenkian Foundation and launched at the same time as Bullying Line, the telephone helpline service provided by ChildLine and reported on by La Fontaine (1991). The booklet was well received by people in education and sold extremely well. Many schools bought multiple copies to distribute to members of the teaching staff and support staff and governors; and it was the interest shown by schools that provided the genesis of an idea. Why not invite schools which have started anti-bullying programmes to share their ideas and approaches with colleagues in other schools — teachers writing for teachers. From our files it was possible to identify a number of schools which had bought multiple copies and were in the process of developing their various approaches. Understandably some were more advanced than others. Drawing upon the schools who were willing to become involved in the project, it was necessary to invite a representative cross-section to take part. Schools were chosen from the maintained and non-maintained sectors. There are primary, middle and secondary schools; rural and urban schools; big schools and small schools; plus single sex, denominational and multi-ethnic schools. It was thought that having such a wide-ranging list would enable other schools to identify with the approaches employed by more than one comparable school in the project.

The book is divided into five sections: management, curriculum, transition, using outside agencies and local authorities. It will be evident that these are not independent or discrete *themes*, as we have called them, but interrelated and interconnected sections. In fact, each of the projects would fit just as well into more than one theme but the editors have placed each report into what they regard as the main theme adopted by a school. Within each theme, schools have adopted their own *approaches* to counter bullying but an internal coherence will be evident from the strategies they adopted.

Awareness of the problem is growing

In the summer of 1987 one of the editors (DT) was invited to give a talk at a Council of Europe conference held in Stavanger, Norway. The subject of the conference was bullying and DT was invited to draw out any connections between disruptive behaviour and bullying. That is, aggression towards teachers and aggression towards peers. In 1987 the literature on disruptive behaviour was extensive but there was very little written on bullying in the United Kingdom. All teachers were aware of the problem at a crisis-management level but no-one had seriously addressed it as a persistent, national problem. Representatives from other European countries also confirmed that the UK was not alone in failing to take bullying seriously. Delegates at the conference learned that the Norwegians had a national anti-bullying campaign, which had started in 1983 following the suicide of three adolescent boys who had been victimised.

In the next five years there was significant progress. In December 1988 the first book on bullying was published in the UK — *Bullying in Schools* (Tattum & Lane). Other initiatives have emerged — none more important than the involvement of the Calouste Gulbenkian Foundation. The Foundation has supported numerous projects to do with bullying, most significantly funding the publication of the booklet *Bullying: a Positive Response. Advice for Parents, Governors and Staff in Schools* (Tattum & Herbert, 1990). In April 1992 the Foundation, in conjunction with British Telecom, funded a national anti-bullying campaign in the UK, when copies of the booklet, together with *Bullying. A Child's View* (La Fontaine, 1991) and *Governors and Bullying* (ACE, 1990) were sent to every maintained and non-maintained school. One of the Foundation's latest initiatives has been to support this publication as part of its continuing association with the booklet and its concern about the problem of bullying.

The Government too has gradually accepted that bullying is a serious and widespread problem in our schools. In March 1989 the Elton Committee published its report on 'Discipline in Schools'. Unfortunately, only three of its 138 recommendations were concerned with bullying. But this was the beginning of an official recognition that bullying was a serious disciplinary problem and the Report correctly placed the issue at the centre of the development of a positive and healthy communal school life:

> A positive school atmosphere involves a sense of community. This sense of community cannot be achieved if a school does not take seriously bad behaviour which mainly affects pupils rather than teachers. It should be clear to pupils that such behaviour is a serious offence against the school community which will be punished. **We therefore recommend that teachers and staff should:**
>
> 66.1 **be alert to signs of bullying and racial harassment;**
>
> 66.2 **deal firmly with all such behaviour; and**
>
> 66.3 **take action based on clear rules which are backed by appropriate sanctions and systems to protect and support victims.**
> (Elton Report, 1989)

In 1991 the DES also commissioned research from Sheffield University aimed at developing strategies to combat bullying. They also funded the Boarding School Line (La Fontaine & Morris, 1992). Even more significantly, the DFE has taken a firm line on the countering of bullying, as this statement by the Schools Minister conveys:

> Schools should be in no doubt about the importance the Government attaches to the eradication of bullying, wherever and whenever it

appears. Bullying is a very unpleasant practice which schools must deal with firmly. It puts the personal well-being and the educational attainment of victims at risk. (Eric Forth in DES NEWS, 18th May 1992)

Looking into bullying will also be a required function of the new inspection teams to be set up by the DFE. In their consultative document, *Framework for the Inspection of Schools* (June 1992), under the section on 'The Quality of the School as a Community — Behaviour and Discipline', inspection teams will be expected to gather evidence on 'the views of parents, teachers and pupils on the incidence of bullying', and their report should include a statement on bullying and the school's policy and practice to counter it.

'Where bullying is considered by parents and/or pupils to be a significant problem, the report should indicate this and evaluate the steps which the school takes to deal with it.' (DFE, June 1992)

These national initiatives, private and public, are very important. Firstly, they raise public, professional and political awareness about the nature, extent and severity of bullying in schools. Secondly, they are positive responses in that they offer schools a variety of ways to tackle the problem. This book is the third stage in the tackling of the problem, because it describes how several schools across the UK have actually put into operation their own policies and practices. This is a most significant step within any campaign for, although there are similarities between schools, each school is different and must work out its own strategies drawing upon the experience of others.

What is bullying?

It is difficult to understand why the education community in general has taken so long to acknowledge that bullying is a serious problem. All who have attended schools as pupils and teachers know that it exists — and many people have distressing stories to tell about their own or their family's experiences. Can it be that bullying is regarded as an inevitable part of school life, with its initiation ceremonies, boisterous play, gang games and teasing? In fact, Rigby & Slee (1990) suggest that there are features in the school environment that harden the attitudes of children towards victims — maybe its competitive ethos. Adults are also prone to dismiss it with hollow clichés, such as 'boys will be boys', 'they've got to learn to look after themselves' and 'it will prepare them for the real world'. Yet how many adults would tolerate abuse and harassment in their workplace without making a complaint? Pupil victims are also reluctant to tell their parents or teachers for

4

fear of making the bullying worse. They are ashamed of what is happening to them, as they often believe that they are the only one singled out for such treatment. This causes them to think that there really is something wrong with them and in extreme cases assume an attitude of self-reproach and guilt. This low perception of self is damaging and can remain with a child into adolescence and adulthood (Tattum & Tattum, 1992b).

In their study into the self-concept of 783 children between 7 and 13 years, O'Moore & Hillery (1991) found that children who were victims of bullying had low self-esteem, and saw themselves in negative terms of being troublesome, more anxious, less popular, and less happy and satisfied than children who had never been bullied. The authors also found that bullies too held feelings of low self-worth in relation to intellectual and school status.

Also, bullying affects the other children who witness the violence and aggression and the consequent distress of the victim. What is more, less aggressive pupils can be drawn into the taunting and tormenting of victims, by group pressure and other social psychological factors. They also know how quickly the direction of the attack can change, for you cannot intimidate and oppress one person without making others afraid.

> Bullying can adversely affect the atmosphere of a class or even the climate of a school. Children have a basic right to freedom from pain, humiliation and fear, whether caused by adults or other children. Schools have a responsibility to create a secure and safe environment for children who are in their care so that parents may hand their children over in the confident knowledge that they will be protected from the bullies (Tattum & Tattum, 1992b).

There is need for us to examine what we understand to be bullying behaviour, for we have in the past held too narrow and simplistic a view. There is also a belief that because bullying is by its very nature a secretive activity, done away from the eyes of adults, there is little that teachers can do to reduce its occurrence. In fact, a number of studies reflect the under-estimation by teachers of bullying when compared with self and peer reports by pupils.

In the following section we shall consider the complexity of the interaction between bully and bullied by looking at its nature, extent, frequency and intensity. But first we turn to the Elton Report (1989) to demonstrate that teachers in that survey were well aware of the behaviour in their classrooms and about the school. The table on page 6 combines data extracted from Tables 1, 2, 9 and 10 of the Report, which deals specifically with bullying.

Table:
THE ELTON REPORT: SHEFFIELD UNIVERSITY SURVEY
Bullying behaviour observed at least once during the survey week
(October 1988)

Primary School Teachers (n = 1200)

Types of bullying behaviour towards other pupils	In class (%)	About school (%)
Physical assaults: eg. pushing, punching, striking	74	86
Verbal abuse: eg. offensive or insulting remarks	55	71

Secondary School Teachers (n = 3200)

Types of bullying behaviour towards other pupils	In class (%)	About school (%)
Physical assaults: eg. pushing, punching, striking	42	66
Verbal abuse: eg. offensive or insulting remarks	62	76

Nature of Bullying

There are a number of definitions of bullying and the following by Roland (1988) is comprehensive:

Bullying is long-standing violence, physical or psychological, conducted by an individual or a group and directed against an individual who is not able to defend himself(sic) in the actual situation.

In addition we offer a very short definition because it enables us to emphasise two particular factors in bully-victim interaction.

Bullying is a wilful, conscious desire to hurt another and put him/her under stress (Tattum, 1988).

We offer the above short definition because it focuses on two important aspects of the interactive nature of bullying. Firstly, it draws attention to the fact that bullies know what they are doing and that it is wrong. In our view

6

accidental or unwitting, hurtful action would not constitute bullying — with one proviso, unless it was perceived to be so by the victim. Bullies get satisfaction from holding power over another less aggressive and vulnerable person. From the victim's point of view, stress is created not only by what actually happens but by the threat and fear of what may happen. The bully does not have to be physically present for a child to be anxious and distressed — the victim might not sleep, might dread going to school, suffer tummy upsets or headaches, peer around corners or not use the school toilets for fear of meeting the bully or bullies.

Bullying can be of a physical or verbal nature, but it can also take the form of other psychologically damaging behaviour such as intimidation, extortion, exclusion, spreading malicious rumours and threatening gestures. Physical bullying can range in severity from a punch to an assault with a dangerous weapon, as in the case of Darren Coulborn, who murdered Ahmed Ullah, a 13 year old Asian boy, in the playground of Burnage High School in 1986. (A report on the Inquiry by Ian Macdonald QC can be found in Macdonald et al., 1989.) Verbal abuse can also range from teasing and taunting to abusive comments about appearance, which can be emotionally bruising. Racial and sexual harassment are particularly insidious forms of bullying, as they attack the most fundamental characteristics of a person's being — their sense of self. In his study of the primary school playground, Blatchford (1989) expresses concern about racism during playtimes, and not only the behaviour of children, which often reflects parental prejudices, but also the attitudes of mid-day supervisors. Unfortunately, teachers too can give support to racist attitudes by the things they say and do (Kelly & Cohn, 1988).

Extent, frequency and intensity of bullying

The most comprehensive survey into the incidence of bullying was carried out in Norway in 1983. It was a nation-wide survey funded by the Ministry of Education and involved some 140,000 junior and senior high school pupils — 8-16 year olds. The results of a self-report questionnaire indicated that approximately 15 percent of children were involved — 9-10 percent victims and 5-6 percent bullies. If we convert this percentage to state schools in the UK, where we have a school population of about 8.6 million, it amounts to the disturbing figure of around 1.3 million pupils involved. In the independent sector 15 percent would represent some 87,000 children and young people. The growing body of research in the UK, mainly small-scale, local studies, indicates that a higher proportion of pupils are involved in our schools and this is confirmed by the reports of schools which conducted surveys as part of this project.

Confirmatory data can be found in the Newson and Newson (1984) longitudinal study which reported that out of a sample of 700 eleven year olds, the mothers of 26 percent were aware that their children were being bullied at school, 4 percent seriously, and another 22 percent were being bullied in the street. In Scotland Mellor (1990), who used a similar definition and questionnaire to the Norwegian survey, produced similar figures to Norway, namely, 9 percent victims and 6 percent bullies. On the other hand, a number of other studies, using virtually the same instruments, provide even more disturbing figures. From a study of 2,000 pupils in middle/secondary schools in South Yorkshire, Ahmed & Smith (1989) found that one in five had been bullied and one in ten had bullied others. Similar findings for secondary schools were reported by Yates and Smith (1989), which involved 234 pupils in two secondary schools, also in the South Yorkshire area.

Of interest to primary schools is the work of Stephenson and Smith (1988). In their 1982 survey in 26 schools in Cleveland they collected data from 49 teachers on 1,078 final year primary school children. Teachers indicated that 23 percent of their children were involved in bullying — 7 percent victims, 10 percent bullies and 6 percent in the dual role of bully and victim. In a later study of 143 children in the top two year groups in one primary school the researchers found a 'high level of agreement between nominations made by teacher and children in the study as to which children were involved in bullying (correlation = .8)'. Similar high levels of agreement were also found by Olweus (1978). These disturbingly high figures suggest that in excess of 1 in 5 primary school children are involved in bullying behaviour.

Some of the data from other countries show evidence of figures comparable with those in England. In a study in Toronto, Canada, of 211 students from 14 classes (grades 4 to 8) it was found that 20 percent were bullied 'now and then' and 'weekly or more often' (Ziegler & Rosenstein-Manner, 1991). An interesting feature of this project is that the researchers also asked the children's parents and teachers about whether they were aware of how often children in the school were bullied. In both cases there was an underestimation compared with the students' experiences. Fourteen percent of parents were aware that their child had been bullied 'now and then' or 'weekly or more often'; and when their teachers were asked, 'How many students in your class have been bullied at least once a week in school this term?', as many as 14 percent replied zero (compared with 6 percent students) and 7 percent just 'didn't know'. Also, using a self-report questionnaire, Rigby & Slee (1990) surveyed 676 pupils in three primary schools and one high school in Adelaide, Australia, and found that when they pooled the responses to the question: 'How often have you been bullied?', for the

8

categories 'pretty often' and 'very often', the figures were 17 percent for boys and 11 percent for girls.

Regardless of which figures we accept, the proportions of children involved are far too high for any complacency. They must be of concern to all who work with children, showing as they do, a very large number of unhappy children in our schools, both victims and bullies, who need help from teachers, parents and other professional groups. It is a strength of this book that it offers a range of approaches; in many instances pupils themselves were involved in developing and sustaining their school's anti-bullying programme.

Long-term effects of bullying

Evidence strongly suggests that bullying tends to be an inter-generational problem. In a 22-year longitudinal study carried out in the USA, Eron and his associates (1987) found that young bullies have about a one in four chance of having a criminal record by age thirty, whilst other children have a one in twenty chance of becoming adult criminals. The researchers studied 870 children from age eight to age 30. Of the 427 children traced at age nineteen, those who had been most aggressive as young children were more likely to have dropped out of school and have delinquent records. Of the 409 who were traced at age 30 most tended to have children who were bullies, to abuse their wives and children, and to have more convictions for violent crimes.

In Norway, Olweus (1989) also writes of bullying as a 'component of a more generally anti-social and rule-breaking behaviour pattern'. From his follow-up studies he found that:

> Approximately 60% of boys who were characterised as bullies in grades 6-9 had at least one court conviction at the age of 24. Even more dramatically, as much as 35-40% of the former bullies had three or more court convictions at this age while this was true of only 10% of the control boys (those who were neither bullies nor victims in grades 6-9). Thus, as young adults the former bullies had a four-fold increase in the level of relatively serious, recidivist criminality (Olweus, 1989).

It is evident that bullying is a serious problem which we can no longer ignore or dismiss. It is a pattern of destructive behaviour which, if not changed, will have disastrous consequences for subsequent generations of children and society at large. Aggressive behaviour is learned. Living with parents who abuse them teaches children that aggression and violence are effective and acceptable means to dominate others and get your own way. For the victim the long-term consequences are also distressing, especially if the experience persists over a long period. Victims often feel isolated by their experience and wonder what is wrong with them that they should be singled out. They may even begin to feel that they deserve the taunts, teasing and harassment so that they become withdrawn and less willing to take social, intellectual or vocational risks. In extreme cases they take these feelings of inadequacy into adult life. Their feeling of self-reproach is part of the reason why they are reluctant to confide in their parents or teachers.

Developing a whole-school approach

If we are effectively to begin to counter the problem of bullying, we need to acknowledge its prevalence and understand more fully its origins and motivation. It is a secretive activity so we need strategies which approach the issues in other ways than the present reactive, crisis-management response, strategies which aim to change attitudes towards bullying while at the same time creating a school ethos that will not tolerate the oppression of one member by another. The aim must be for a whole-school policy which is consistent with the daily experiences of teachers, pupils and parents. Individual schools must look to heighten the awareness of teaching and non-teaching staff so that they are more alert to the extent of bullying and its long-term effects on both parties. This may require a survey to convince some teachers of its prevalence and frequency in their school.

At the centre of its whole-school approach, a school must have a policy on how it may be tackled and reduced. To this end a policy statement must be drawn up and communicated to all parents and pupils. The Governing Body should be involved in its preparation and reiteration, as the 1986 and 1988 Education Acts charge them with legal responsibility for the conduct and discipline of the school. The Advisory Centre for Education has produced an invaluable information sheet on *Governors and Bullying* (ACE, 1990).

The five themes presented in subsequent chapters — management, curriculum, transition, education agencies and local authorities — demonstrate the component parts of a whole- school programme and illustrate that though the process may be different the outcomes are fundamentally the same. Central to all five themes and their approaches is management, because it is not enough to have a policy unless it is sustained and reiterated throughout each school year. Bullying will not be reduced by a one-off project; rather the condemnation of bullying must be an integral part of the school ethos.

This section develops some of the *reasons* why a school needs a whole-school policy statement. The reasons and elements have been developed through working with the various schools and other organisations. (See Tattum & Tattum, 1992b for further discussion of these points.)

Reasons

1. *To counter the view that bullying is an inevitable part of school life* — and so challenge teachers' and pupils' attitudes towards aggressive behaviour and examine their relationships with each other, not just pupil-pupil but also teacher-teacher and teacher-pupil relationships. A school has to decide whether it 'unintentionally' reinforces or discourages aggressive behaviour.

2. *To move beyond a crisis-management approach* which only reacts to critical cases and permits some headteachers to deny that bullying happens in their school. The *elements* discussed later will enable a school to progress into a more preventative ethos.

3. *To open up discussion at all levels* from a full staff development day to class/tutorial groups. In this way bullying will no longer be looked upon as a secret activity affecting the few.

4. *To involve more people in the identification and condemnation of bullying.* In their 1982 survey Stephenson and Smith made a study of six primary schools with the highest and six primary schools with the lowest incidence of bullying. 'In all but one of the low bullying schools the teachers expressed articulate, considered and also purposeful views on bullying which emphasised the need for prevention whereas this was less apparent in the high bullying schools. The responses suggest that there was an agreed policy on bullying in the low bullying schools' (Stephenson & Smith, 1988).

5. *To draw up an agreed set of procedures for staff to follow when enquiring into a case of bullying.* For it is only when documented profiles are produced that a school will be able to isolate bullying individuals and break up bullying gangs. It is also better if procedures are drawn up, since it is much easier to deal with confrontations about discipline in a calm atmosphere before there is a difficult incident, if there are agreed ground-rules.

6. *To create a supportive climate and break down the code of secrecy.* When bullying is reported by pupils or parents it *must* be taken seriously and acted upon in a way which discourages the bully without humiliating the victim. Children are reluctant to tell because they fear the consequences, not only from the bully but also from adults. We must avoid blaming the victim for the bully's aggressive behaviour.

7. *To provide a safe, secure learning environment for all pupils* — for this is the right of every child and young person attending our schools and colleges. Pupils cannot satisfactorily do their work if they are burdened with anxiety, humiliation and fear. Lothian's Children's Charter gives substance to this basic entitlement (see pages 176).

11

Elements

1. *A policy statement declaring the unacceptability of bullying.* This statement should be collectively drawn up by staff including non-teachers and governors, so that all adults directly associated with the school feel that they have been involved in the school's anti-bullying declaration and so are committed to its implementation. The same points apply to pupils, who must also be part of the process, as occurs in the following reports by schools. The statement should begin by positively expressing the school's standards and expectations, and then identify those behaviours which will not be tolerated and the consequences for anyone who persistently breaches the statement.

   Research demonstrates that aggression in children can manifest itself in different ways and towards different targets. In school it can mean bullying, disruption, vandalism and theft. Therefore, a school which sets out to counter bullying will also have a positive effect on reducing other forms of anti-social behaviour (Olweus, 1989). Another positive outcome reported by Olweus is that truancy is reduced because children are no longer afraid to attend school and actually express greater satisfaction with school life.

2. *A multi-level approach involving a wide range of people.* It is important that teaching and non-teaching staff are involved in the discussions and implementation of an anti- bullying programme. Most bullying takes place around the school premises — in the playground, toilets, dinner queues and in a variety of other locations. It takes place during school hours at times when pupils are less closely supervised. Therefore, to counter the secretive element of bullying every school should involve all employees who are not teachers. The model 'Spheres of Involvement' (page 186) illustrates the wide range of people who can work with the school as part of its whole-school (even community) approach to bullying. At the centre of the model are teachers, pupils and parents.

3. *The development of short, medium and long-term strategies.* The importance of this element is evident from the work done in each of the schools. Their evaluations are cautiously expressed as each recognises that bullying will be significantly reduced only if their anti-bullying programme is sustained. In element one, examples were given of the successes achieved as a result of the Norwegian nation-wide intervention campaign. The main components of this campaign, which was aimed at teachers, parents and pupils, were a 32-page booklet for *all* parents, and a survey of schools. In Bergen there was a 50 percent decrease in bully/victim problems during the two years following the campaign, for both boys and girls (Olweus, 1989). Although more

cautious in his analysis of data gathered in Stavanger, Roland (1988) supports the finding that there was a reduction in bullying problems in schools which displayed a general *commitment* to the use of the materials and programmes. As described earlier in this chapter (page 2), we too have a nation-wide initiative in the UK. What we lack is a national or regional evaluation of the success of the intervention programmes.

4. *A wide discussion of bullying to open up the issues and tackle what is a complex problem.* The reasons for wider discussion have already been rehearsed. In order to counter bullying there needs to be a detailed set of guidelines for teachers and other school staff, plus parents, governors and pupils. Detailed guidelines for each of these groups is provided in *Bullying: A Positive Response* (Tattum & Herbert 1990).

5. *An anti-bullying campaign integrated within the school curriculum.* If we are to tackle bullying behaviour at a school-wide level then it is not sufficient to focus only on one-off periods in a pastoral or PSE programme. Nor can it be left to occasional exhortations in morning assembly. The curriculum, both formal and informal, is a vehicle for influencing pupils' perceptions, attitudes and values. Therefore, we must use it in a planned way within a whole-school response to the problem of bullying.

Theme two is about 'Using the Curriculum' to counter bullying and in the theme about transition between schools Lakeside Primary also deals extensively with ways of employing the curriculum to challenge pupils' attitudes towards aggression. On pages 80-84 the editors develop in greater detail their views on how the school curriculum can be used as a vehicle for change in the area of bullying.

Theme One

Management Strategies

Introduction

The tackling of bullying in school is rightly one of the functions of management. It is a management problem. There will always be teachers who act individually to counter bullying whenever they come across it among their pupils. However, the work of an enthusiastic or committed teacher is insufficient to tackle the enormous problem of bullying in schools. If attempts to combat bullying are carried out on an occasional basis, reacting to the problem only when it occurs, then, inevitably, it will recur, for it will be merely a matter of luck which child is with which member of staff, or who spots that bullying is going on.

As the approaches adopted by the schools here show, the countering of bullying is a wide-ranging exercise. Although each began at different stages of their development, their attempts at countering the problem are remarkably similar. At Glapton Primary School, for example, it was through the production of a school behaviour policy that the threads of improving behaviour, developing the Personal and Social Education (PSE) programme and countering bullying were drawn together. The policy was written as a set of tasks to be performed.

At Shirehampton Infant School, the approach was slightly different. An unpleasant incident, followed by the staff's powerlessness to advise the

15

parents, was the spur to tackle the problem of bullying. The staff here were also developing a PSE programme and their work took them into the curriculum itself.

At Exwick Middle School, the staff were already practised in developing and implementing policies relating to the curriculum, administration and the support of teaching and learning resources. Bullying rose to the top of their agenda following media attention and the attendance of a member of staff at a conference in Sheffield. Building on existing good practices, the school was able to incorporate a programme aimed at minimising bullying.

Eastbourne Comprehensive School began with the appointment of new senior staff and a radical shake-up of the school's management structures. The staff were asked to consider the aims of the school and these aims were collected into the grandly titled 'Vision for Eastbourne School'. The attempts at countering bullying in this school sprang from the need to tackle Equality of Opportunity issues. The staff became aware of the problems surrounding inter-personal skills and, with help from a member of the LEA's advisory team, the initiative was begun.

Wycliffe College was stimulated to act positively on bullying by the concern shown in the media. The work was given extra impetus by the attendance of a member of staff at a day conference organised by the Gloucester Police Community Service Department and the address given by one of the co-editors. The school has to cope with particular problems posed by being both a boarding school and one which caters for pupils from the age of 4 to the age of 18. Their action plan was set out in eight distinct stages based upon the findings of their own in-school research.

The work developed by St. Mary's C of E Primary School sprang from the need to tackle the problems caused within the playground areas at break and lunchtimes. The lunchtime Organisers were the adults who had to deal with the problems as they arose. The school's response to giving support and guidance to these beleaguered and often undervalued members of the school community completes this collection of management approaches to the tackling of bullying. Together they form a comprehensive study; individually they can offer assistance to similar schools.

1. Glapton Primary School, Nottingham

Chris Elkins, Headteacher

The school is a county primary co-educational school for children aged between three and eleven. There are 380 on roll in ten classes, plus an additional 40 place nursery catering for 80 part-time pupils. The catchment area is mainly from a mixed urban background, the majority of pupils coming from a very large housing estate. The estate comprises a mixture of council owned housing, some housing association houses and some private housing owned mainly by young first time buyers. Although the school has a racial mix, the white population represents a large majority of the pupils.

1.1 The management action plan

The aim was to move to a position beyond the piecemeal reaction of individual teachers to the problem of bullying in school, since that behaviour impinged upon events in the school day. What was required was an ethos where the school was recognised as a place where bullying might happen in the every-day lives of children, but where everyone was committed to tackling it constructively when it did.

Previous experience had shown that tackling a problem area collectively was far more successful than initiatives by an individually committed or gifted teacher trying to enthuse other colleagues. Working towards an agreed goal, using similar methods, sharing ideas and problems, knowing that support was at hand and giving clear signals to pupils throughout the school had proved economical of effort and effective.

Various problem areas such as inter-personal skills, multicultural and racial awareness, equal opportunities, non-accidental injury, sexual abuse and emotional and behavioural difficulties have been the target for attention, as society and its teachers have become aware of the need. It seemed logical to gather several threads together into a whole-school behaviour policy. Bullying has elements in common with many of these problem areas and the strategies which had been successful in the past could be adopted or modified to tackle this problem also.

In the early 1980s the LEA had raised awareness about multicultural issues, including the ways that racism can be embedded in hierarchies, systems and institutions. The bullying associated with racism would probably be best tackled by the whole school institution. For dealing with children exhibiting emotional and behaviourial difficulties, the school has adopted several types of behaviour modification programme, setting the behaviour as the target rather than viewing the child as the problem. This is often a successful strategy, usually involving the Headteacher as well as the parents. This strategy, it was felt, could probably be employed for helping

Management tasks

1. To ensure that the Behaviour Policy is in keeping with any written statement of general principles laid down by the School Body, the LEA Statement of the Curriculum and the General Aims of the school.

2. To establish agreement over the policy with the School Governors and staff.

3. To decide how the policy is to be effected.

4. To ensure that it is applied.

5. To clarify the roles of the Line Management so that there is mutual support.

6. To promote an effective Communication System within the school.

7. When planning, delivering and evaluating the curriculum, to recognise that the quality of its content and the teaching and learning methods through which it is delivered are important influences on pupils' behaviour.

8. To give early warning of developing problems to the Support Service.

9. To monitor school attendance and report problems to the EWO.

10. To actively seek suggestions from the pupils for inclusion in the policy.

11. To communicate the relevant parts of the policy to parents, to invite their comments and seek their support.

12. To promote a positive image locally.

bullies achieve self-control. The school had previously bid into an LEA initiative on Personal and Social Education (PSE). This had followed the observation by staff that a number of pupils had poor inter-personal skills. Staff wished to be more pro-active. Ideas were collated, disseminated and implemented to improve the image of self and of peers to promote positive inter-personal relationships.

Encouraged by the improvement in general behaviour and a calmer, friendlier atmosphere, the publication of the Elton Report (1989) was received with interest. The report was to prove instrumental in both raising appropriate questions and providing routes to some answers. When *Bullying: A Positive Response (1990)* was published, copies were purchased for each member of staff to augment the practical ideas in Personal and Social Education (PSE) and to raise awareness of the prevalence of bullying in even the best regulated schools. This has proved a most useful source book, for it keeps the issue alive and is in constant use.

To draw these separate yet intertwined strands together, a place was allocated in the school management plan for the development of a whole school behaviour policy. The practical implementation of the policy has ensured that the issue of combating bullying is highlighted from the present up to 1995 at least.

1.2 Compiling and implementing the policy

Before beginning the process of drawing up a policy statement, the following questions had to be addressed:

1. Who should be involved in developing it?
2. What should it contain?
3. How should it be implemented?
4. What steps should be taken to review it regularly?

Every school will have different answers to these questions, as the history and circumstances of each differs. For this school, like every school, the answers were particular, but the issues surrounding them apply more generally.

Who should be involved in developing the school behaviour policy?

The Elton Report (1989) indicates that school governors and parents as well as pupils and staff should be involved in this process. However, this posed further questions which had to be addressed:

How committed are we to seeking the views of others?

How can we canvas views most effectively?

Can we develop a questionnaire that is without bias and that will effectively provide the information required?

If we send out such a questionnaire, will it imply that the school has behavioural and discipline problems?

Would a meeting for parents raise issues that might result, however unintentionally, in a loss of confidence in the school?

Are we clear enough in our thinking to brief governors on the issues involved?

Are we confident enough in our management structure and classroom skills to implement the target of an agenda partially set by others?

How interested, informed and committed are these others?

How much time and what resources can be devoted to collating the incoming information, interpreting it and providing feedback?

After consideration of these questions the following action plan was devised:

1. Allocate time in the form of an INSET day and twilight sessions.

2. Decide what the policy should accomplish.

3. Allocate tasks to individuals

What should the behaviour policy contain?

At the beginning it was not at all clear what might be useful content. The materials already to hand (a list of school rules, a list of sanctions, a line management structure) were reassessed. In a brain-storming session, staff produced ideas and took decisions about who should develop these further. The ideas raised practical implications which were addressed before tackling the next issue. Sometimes in addressing a practical matter, the next issue suggested itself.

After a lengthy process, the following sections were developed to answer the question 'what should the behaviour policy contain?'

- It should promote the general aims of the school
- It should identify management tasks
- It should have a clear system of affirmation so that positive approval and praise are more in evidence than a system of sanctions
- It should have a clear system of sanctions, outlining roles and responsibilities where necessary and indicating the legal requirements

A code of conduct for pupils

There are a great many people in a school so we need rules to allow everyone to work properly, safely and enjoyably.

You are expected to behave well which means doing nothing that is inconsiderate of others.

Teachers are in the position of parents/guardians while you are in school. This means in particular that:

- There is no excuse for rudeness, disrespect or insolence towards any staff and parent helpers etc. in school.
- You should do as you are told at once and without argument.

In the classroom

- Keep your own belongings tidy.
- Pack things away neatly when an activity is finished.
- When your teacher talks to the whole class keep quiet and concentrate.
- If the class is asked a question put your hand up to answer. Do not call out unless asked for quick ideas.
- Do not distract others when they are working.
- Do not bring toys or sweets/biscuits or jewellery to school, unless the teacher allows it on special occasions.
- If you have to carry breakable things eg. a milkbottle, carry it in a basket.
- If you have to go out of school eg. to the dentist or speech therapist, you must either have a note from your parent or your parent must ring school first.
- Remember to bring your reading book back to school.
- Make sure you have your PE and swimming kit at school on the right days. You cannot go home for it.
- If you have been absent remember to bring a note to your teacher.

Around the school

Walk sensibly.

- Make sure your teacher knows where you are.
- When going on a message always take a partner.
- Be quiet in Assemblies and Services.
- Be quiet and stand still when the whistle goes in the yard.
- Play in the yard where the teacher on duty can see you.
- Keep to the paved areas when it is wet and check that your shoes are clean when going inside.
- Use the main entrance nearest your own classroom.
- Keep quiet and walk outside sensibly when the Fire Alarm sounds.
- Put your litter in a bin or keep it in your pocket until you can.
- In icy weather do not make slides.
- If you throw snowballs make sure —
    that they are soft
    that the person you throw at doesn't mind
    that you throw low.

What to do if you are bullied or hit

- Do not hit back or ask someone else to hit for you. If you have a problem or a quarrel ask your teacher to help you sort it out.
- Tell a grown-up in charge ESPECIALLY IF THE OTHER PERSON SAYS THEY WILL DO WORSE THINGS IF YOU TELL.

If the other person bullies you again, tell your teacher or the Headteacher and your parents. Grown-ups can stop bullies but only if you tell them about it.

■ it should outline a code of conduct for pupils. This resulted in the presentation of a handbook for the pupils entitled 'How to Behave at School'.

■ It should outline helpful classroom management strategies

■ It should provide guidance for all adults who interact with children at school

Some exemplars from this policy document are shown.

1. Management tasks (page 18)

2. A code of conduct for pupils (page 21)

How should the school behaviour policy be implemented?

By the time the school behaviour policy had been drafted and practical issues addressed or identified, it was clear in what ways and by whom each section should be implemented. The Headteacher and teachers could see their roles, identify the training needed to develop new skills or further thinking and target the tasks to be carried out. It was also clearer where the governors, support staff, ancillary staff, parents and pupils could also play their parts.

Involving the staff

Programmes for the INSET events for the teachers included:

Discussion of the various forms of bullying; how to free children to discuss bullying; how to improve the self-esteem of bullies and help them to improve their self-control.

Discussion about helping victims to improve their strategies for self-assertiveness and to give support and praise in order to aid their gaining of control of the situation.

Drawing up an equal opportunities statement.

Identifying books displaying bias and withdrawing them from the Infant Library.

Devising a list of means of praising children.

Devising model letters of praise which could be sent home.

Carrying out an audit of the use of time in school so that sufficient time can be allocated to PSE and the personal safety programme, to allow a planned curriculum to be delivered, as well as responding to matters arising in the daily lives of children in school.

Agreeing a method for monitoring the delivery of such a curriculum, to ensure entitlement and a developmental progression.

If you are bullied...

· tell your teacher
· or the head teacher
· and your parent,
Bullies like to frighten people.
They say things like they'll hit you if
you tell. But grown-ups can stop them.

Setting up workshops to organise the content of the PSE and personal safety curricula (specifically including bullying) to reflect a developmental progression.

Involving the school governors

The draft school behaviour policy was presented to the governors for comment, suggestions and adoption. The governors expressed interest in several points and were pleased to adopt it without amendment. The governors were interested particularly in the booklet, 'How to Behave in School' produced with the help of the children, and asked for feedback about developments on a regular basis.

Involving specialist staff including the psychological service

The use of play therapy for both victims and bullies is available in a limited way for teachers from the Local Authority's staff at a special school. This has been used successfully and the school is now considering ways of making this support more widely available. Training for staff in the management of children with emotional/social needs, including behaviour modification programmes, has been available from the schools' psychological service.

Involving ancillary staff

The midday supervisors attended a session at an in-service day to look at the issues arising for them from the section in the policy on 'Guidance for teachers, non-teaching staff and parent-helpers'. In particular they were asked to be alert to signs of bullying, racial harassment and sexual inequality. What these signs might constitute and incidents which had already occurred were discussed. Consideration was given to ways in which they could deal firmly with all such behaviour and protect and support the victims. The necessity of reporting such incidents to their line managers was stressed.

Involving the children

The children responded to the teachers' initiatives in PSE by openly talking about the bullying they had experienced, as victim, bully or spectator. Individuals became more confident about confiding to teachers instances which occurred during the school day.

Staff consulted the children about equal opportunities. Among other matters, the younger children and older girls drew the attention of staff to the domination of the junior playground by the older boys playing football or games which occupied all the space. The girls and younger children were relegated to the periphery. Intrusion into the central area was often met with force, threats or unpleasantness. This issue was raised in all classes and the majority wanted the older boys to allow them access to the central area. An assembly on caring and sharing was followed by an announcement that there was to be equal rights in the playground. This was intended to signal clearly to the older boys that the staff would uphold the rights of all children to the playground space. There was initial objection and some resistance from some boys, who were dealt with according to the guidelines set. PSE sessions addressed the problem and ideas for alternative activities were found.

The code of conduct for the pupils was discussed with all the children. They were asked if they thought it might be helpful if every new pupil was given a copy of 'How to Behave at School'. Their comments and ideas were noted and illustrations designed by the children used to put the message across. The children were very enthusiastic and staff used the booklets for induction at the start of the school year.

Involving the parents

It was decided to involve the parents tacitly at first. This was done by sending home copies of the booklet 'How to Behave at School', accompanied by a letter of explanation. In the booklet, the school mentions bullying explicitly for the first time. The aim was to signal to parents the willingness and ability of the staff to tackle bullying and to enable the parents and their children to feel more powerful in combating the problem should it occur. Staff were given spare copies of the section 'Guidance for teachers, non-teaching staff and parent-helpers' to talk through with parent-helpers as required.

What steps should be taken to review the school behaviour policy regularly?

This form of evaluation should be an item for consideration when compiling the policy document. Without its inclusion, it cannot be known how successful the school's attempts at combating unacceptable behaviour have been. The following are all criteria for success which the school looked for after implementing this policy:

- The staff would initially hear of *more* instances of bullying than at present. This would signal that the children were now more confident they would be listened to, that their problems would be taken seriously and that the staff would take satisfactory action.
- All the adults involved in the initiative would feel confident that they could tackle bullying constructively, focusing on the behaviour rather than viewing the child as the problem.
- Staff would be using similar strategies, sharing ideas and problems as well as seeking support when appropriate.
- Parents would turn to the school for advice or make observations reflecting that they had noted the school's ethos.
- There would be a change in the children's attitudes towards bullying.
- Bullies would succeed in their attempts to change their behaviour to gain more control of it and improve their self-image.
- Victims would succeed in attempts to be more self-assertive and improve their self-image.

The following examples of feedback show that such criteria can be used successfully and one example, although anecdotal, serves to underline many of the criteria of success for which the school was looking.

At a meeting the mid-day supervisors were asked to review the guidelines and to comment about the training they had received. The supervisors reported that they felt well supported and much more confident than previously when tackling the problem in school.

The Headteacher received a letter from a local resident, complaining about the behaviour of some year 3 children. It appeared that they had been annoying local residents in the evenings. The complaint was vague, but the children identified the following behaviour themselves as causing the concern:

1. They had been running into people's gardens, tapping on their doors and windows and running away. The residents were elderly.

2. The dog belonging to one of the children had been fouling gardens and digging holes in the gardens.

3. The children had been making too much noise deliberately to annoy residents.

4. They had been picking on a very young girl and making her cry.

The children were asked how they felt now that the Headteacher knew, especially after the work which had been covered in this area during PSE lessons. They replied that they felt ashamed. They were asked to reflect on the effects of their actions on the other people. This reflection made them sad that their actions had done them no credit. They were then asked what they could do to change so that each could become someone of whom they could be proud and of whom others would say positive things. The ideas which the children came up with were as follows:

1. To play on the Green, not in and out of people's gardens.

2. To leave the dog at home.

3. To list games they like to play which were quieter.

4. To leave the little girl alone, or to play with her if she wanted.

5. To collect litter from the Green.

The Headteacher contacted the complainant to say that action had been taken and requesting information on the children's behaviour after two weeks. At the end of the fortnight the Headteacher sent for the children to ask them to assess their behaviour. They reflected on it realistically. The Headteacher told them that she had received no complaints and that one local resident had called in to thank the children for staying out of her garden and for playing more quietly. She also told them that their class teacher had commented that their behaviour had recently been more thoughtful and kind. They were asked how they felt now. They replied that they felt happy and good about themselves, in marked contrast to their comment two weeks previously. To express how pleased the Headteacher was about their changed behaviour she awarded each a badge which they gladly wore.

One of the children's parents had been to see the Headteacher after the child had told her about the complaints. She was puzzled that the child had not been punished and the parents not informed. She wanted to know who had made the complaints so that she could take her child around to apologise. She also knew that her child did bully and could be a nuisance at times. However, she conceded that punishments and being made to apologise had not worked in the past. After the tactics being used to improve her child's behaviour were explained — the raising of his own expectations of himself and the importance of praise in that process — his mother agreed to support the approach. A letter praising the child's efforts and achievements was later sent home and this gave both parents and child much satisfaction.

This anecdote illustrates an example of the criteria for success sought in the original document. However, this approach could not have succeeded on an ad-hoc basis. It needed the full support of the staff and the governors and the raising of the children's awareness of what could be achieved. In other words, to have any chance of success, it needed a whole school approach.

2. Shirehampton Infant School, Avon

Liz Minson, Headteacher

Different circumstances and events led to a whole school approach by the Shirehampton Infant School in Bristol. It began as an investigation into behaviour, but moved into the unexpected area of the curriculum. The school serves a well established community. The third generation of local families now attend the school. Most of the children — mainly white European— know each other from nursery school or playgroups. It is a settled community. There are 250 pupils on roll and the catchment area is mainly council owned, although some houses are privately owned. Most of the children will remain with their peers through to secondary school. Developing good interpersonal relationships in the peer group is therefore an important part of the curriculum.

We must not assume that bullying does not occur in Infant schools. Children are busy establishing, forming and breaking relationships from an early age. It is part of the socialising process and will continue throughout the pupils' school careers. If a pupil develops a negative self-image at an

Below: Parents helping to solve a problem.

early age in this school, it may follow him or her for the rest of his or her school career. When young children are observed in their play, they can be seen to be experimenting socially: they are learning how to become an accepted member of their peer group and will draw on models they observe elsewhere. As teachers and parents, we need to challenge the negative images which some pupils carry with them. The children also need to be given the opportunity to talk about the ways in which they behave and learn that their behaviour affects others.

One unpleasant bullying incident developed into something serious when it carried on outside school. The member of staff who was made aware of the problem felt unable to give advice to the parents or the child. The problem was aired in a staff meeting. Individual members of staff began to discuss this incident and similar ones they had encountered. It soon became clear that there were very differing views about how to deal with bullying. There was no consistent approach. This must have been confusing for children, since their subsequent treatment depended upon the member of staff who dealt with the incident. The staff felt powerless to give advice. Further, if they as adults felt powerless, how much worse the feelings of children being bullied. The staff, both teaching and non-teaching, spent many hours discussing the nature of the problem and then decided on a six point plan:

1. Appropriate materials were acquired to help the staff focus on the issue.

2. Concern was widened to include governors and midday supervisors. It was felt that everyone involved with the children needed to be aware of the problem, particularly those on duty in the playground.

3. A PSE programme was already in existence and it was decided to include some work on countering bullying in the programme.

4. Strategies were sought to help the adults in school deal with bullying in a way which showed concern for all parties involved.

5. Strategies to enable individual children to feel secure were also sought.

6. An atmosphere where children could feel that adults would listen to their concerns and treat seriously what they said was also identified as being desirable.

2.1 Implementing the plan

Awareness of the issues had now been brought to the attention of the staff. Staff attended appropriate INSET courses, for example a Teacher Effectiveness Training course which helped the staff to become effective, active listeners as well as improving their classroom management techniques. The headteacher sought out other schools in the area which had bullying on their agendas and shared problems and concerns. One of the objectives of the PSE programme is 'a healthy mind in a healthy body' and this lent itself to tackling bullying. As a staff we now felt it appropriate to share our concerns with the parents; we wanted to bring the bullying issue out into the open. Parents were therefore invited to an open evening to discuss the PSE issues in school. Bullying was one of those issues. The staff strategies were explained to parents and the aims were expressed as follows:

1. To create a better atmosphere for the children.
2. To give the children strategies to cope with anti-social behaviour from their peers and adults if that were the case.
3. To inform parents of any incidents that occurred.

Furthermore, we stressed the importance of working together as a team and our hope that together the strategies would be reinforced.

Staff were concerned lest parents' comments along the lines of, 'I tell him to thump them back,' 'Do to her what she did to you,' or, 'What's wrong with my child that he won't hit back?' were not going to help the staff's efforts to develop the child's self- esteem and self respect. To assist the staff programme, parents were informed termly about which aspects of the

Below: Working together.

CHILDREN'S ANTI-BULLYING STATEMENT

Bullying is hurting someone emotionally, physically or both, with a group of people, or one more powerful person against another person.

HOW CAN WE HELP

VICTIM

- Tell a teacher (or parent) .
- Ignore the bully if possible.
- Walk away.
- Tell bully's parents.
- Discuss problem with bully.
- Stay with safe friends.

BULLY

- Is there anything you do to others that is hurtful or upsetting?
- Think of what you are doing to the victim (or victims).
- Think better of it.
- Stop it.

OBSERVERS

- Don't watch the fight (or argument) or you will encourage the bully more.
- Don't copy the bully.
- Don't take the bully's side.
- Tell someone. (Friends, teacher, parents).
- Don't encourage the bully.
- Don't let the bully hang around with you.

STATEMENT

Bullying everywhere should be stopped because it's very disturbing and hurtful both emotionally and physically.

ANTI-BULLYING POLICY

Guidelines for Parents

What is bullying?

Bullying is threatening or dominating behaviour towards another person with the calculated intention to hurt or frighten them physically, emotionally or psychologically. It is usually, but not always, repetitive. Children have the right to receive their education free from such humiliation, oppression and abuse.

What to do in the event of bullying

1. *Watch for signs of distress in your children. There could be an unwillingness to attend school, a pattern of headaches or stomach aches, equipment that has gone missing, a request for extra pocket money, damaged clothing or bruising.*

2. *Discuss an active interest in the child's social life. Discuss friendships, how playtime is spent and the journeys to and from school.*

3. *If you think your child is being bullied inform the school immediately and ask for an interview with the member of staff who should deal with the incident.*

4. *Tell your son or daughter that there is nothing wrong with him/her. He/she is not the only victim.*

5. *Advise your son or daughter not to hesitate to tell an adult, for example a liked and trusted teacher.*

6. *Advise you son or daughter not to try and buy the bully off with sweets or other 'presents', and not to give in to demands for money.*

7. *Keep a written record if the bullying persists. It will be painful but it will provide supportive evidence regarding WHO, WHAT, WHERE AND WHEN.*

8. *Together with an appointed teacher and your son or daughter work out a plan of action. Should the bullying be repeated the plan must be followed and an adult told that it has happened again.*

What if you child is a bully?

If you think your child may be bullying others, do contact us, so that together we can solve the problem.

With acknowledgements to *Bullying: A Positive Response.*

33

programme the school was going to cover and how this related to their children so that parents could reinforce it at home. Parents had and still have the opportunity to examine all the materials that their children will be using: the videos, books outlining aspects of the programme and books supporting the themes, available in the school library. Parents have shown that they are pleased to be involved in this area of their child's education. Parents are also given the opportunity to withdraw their child from any aspect of the programme. No-one has as yet done so.

Parents were also informed of how staff would tackle bullying at school. Bullying is sometimes taken as a theme in assemblies. This has to be done sensitively. However, through role-play or the use of puppets, a point can be emphasised or children's capacities to empathise developed. Class assemblies often highlight a problem that is of concern to the children and spring from their discussions. Class story times and review sessions are used to discuss incidents as they occur and the children grow used to discussing their feelings, so that negative ones can be changed. The school has recently made its own video entitled 'A Day in the Life of a Reception Child at Shirehampton Infant School'. Part of this deals explicitly with bullying in the context of the PSE programme and is available to the parents.

2.2 Evaluation

To identify objective criteria in such a developmental programme is perhaps to reduce to statistical criteria the affective area of education. However, examples of the kinds of behaviour that the school is trying to promote are available and the gathering and recording of incidents acts as an incentive to everyone involved with the school.

It is possible to give young children small but effective strategies to deal with anti-social behaviour. They can be heard saying 'I don't have to listen to that,' or 'That makes me sad.' In the playground, an effective technique is to stamp feet and shout 'No!' as loudly as possible, as recommended by Elliott (1991). Children know that adults or other children will react positively to their distress. Noting snatches of conversation such as, 'We don't do that here,' has a reinforcing effect on the whole programme. The vast majority of children, who are not involved in bullying, can become a positive force in the protection of those who are involved, by giving support to the victim and advising the bully to stop.

As the strategies evolved by the staff are noted and seen to be successful, so the caring ethos of the school becomes strengthened. The effect on the school has been considerable. The whole school approach has been a unifying factor, not only amongst the staff but also amongst members of the community. The PSE programme has led to a wider sharing of curriculum issues. The governors feel their input is valued and parents can see the governors working for the development of the whole child. Parents themselves feel they are being treated as partners and become involved in a variety of ways in the school.

In the process of administering the Standard Assessment Tasks and collecting evidence for the Teacher Assessment, many of the activities have to be carried out through group work. Children have learned to encourage and value the contributions of others far more than before. Even the least articulate of the children are drawn into the discussions.

Importantly, the children's language development is increasing as they learn new vocabulary to express their feelings. This last area is worth considering in much greater detail. It is an area which can be effectively measured and the positive effects of an anti-bullying campaign in the school can be charted.

3. Exwick Middle School, Exeter

Ken Turner, Headteacher

Exwick Middle School also took a management approach to solving the problem of bullying. The school is a County Middle school with 240 pupils on roll aged from 8 to 12, in educational years 3 to 7. The catchment area is made up of mainly owner-occupiers and predominantly first time buyers. However, the catchment area is changing, for there are some significant developments in Housing Associations. The majority of the pupils come from white European backgrounds.

A school management plan was already in existence concerning the curriculum, administration, the support of learning and teaching and resources. Three policies had already been developed concerning the management of disruptive behaviour, aggressive behaviour in school and a thematic approach to respect in the school. There was also a developing approach to PSE in the school based upon the guidelines set out in the National Curriculum (Circular 6). It was acknowledged that further policies needed to be developed and incorporated into the life of the school. However, the staff had some expertise in the development of such policies, and lessons learned from previous exercises could be applied to similar problems. The idea of tackling bullying as an issue came from a number of sources, for example the increasing attention given to the problem of the media, news of the research taking place at Sheffield University and the Deputy Headteacher's attendance at a day conference.

The staff had no idea of the extent of the problem in the school. To gain an insight into the nature of the behaviour as it affected Exwick, it was decided to carry out a questionnaire to act as an initial audit. The children administered the survey, so their attention was drawn to the fact that the staff took one of their problems seriously and awareness of the problem was generally heightened. The survey revealed that 28 children were currently victims of bullying:

Year 4:	9
Year 5:	7
Year 6:	8
Year 7:	4
Total:	28

This represented about 12% of the school population and once this was known the staff were eager to establish strategies to overcome the problem.

Following extensive discussions, the staff resolved to produce three sets of guidelines, one for pupils, one for parents and one for staff. The children's guidelines were developed in conjunction with the children, thereby rein-

PLAYGROUND SURVEY

Lower School Summary

		YES	NO
1	Do you enjoy break-time outside at the moment?	14%	86%
2.	Are you happy with the way time on the pitch is organised?	57%	43%
3.	Does football improve breaktimes?	19%	81%
4.	Would you want breaktimes to be organised differently?	71%	29%

Upper School Summary

1.	Do you enjoy breaktimes?	66%	34%
2.	Do you use the pitch	75%	25%
3.	Are you happy with the current arrangements?	75%	25%

forcing the idea that staff were taking the problem seriously. The parents' guidelines, written by staff, tried to put the problem in perspective and offer practical advice taken from *Bullying: A Positive Response.* The staff guidelines developed out of these two. All parents and children were given these leaflets.

Inevitably, the number of incidents reported rose. This is to be expected as children and parents test the system. As many of the incidents which caused problems occurred at break and lunchtime, the staff felt that they needed to know exactly what was happening and how they could all work to prevent unpleasantness. Break and lunchtime should be a positive experience for everyone involved. INSET time was allocated to two members of staff, along with meal-time assistants, to attend a course organised by the Educational Psychologists and also attended by other schools in the area tackling similar problems.

From that course a number of initiatives ensued. First, the organisation of lunchtime and the role of the assistants was examined. Each year group was allocated an assistant who could then grow to know the pupils. The geography of the school helps this process, since the year groups can be effectively isolated within the school building. Some organisational changes were made which helped the smooth running of the process of feeding the children. Parents were informed of the changes and the reasons behind them.

Secondly, the staff turned their attention to the problems posed and opportunities afforded by play areas. The staff needed to know how the play areas were being used and what the pupils' attitudes were to the play areas.

The pupils were canvassed for their opinions. The results of the survey revealed some surprising figures.

If the school was to develop a caring ethos then the obvious disparities between the attitudes of the upper and lower schools would not continue to operate in ways that many younger pupils were experiencing. A particular problem was the matter of space and the playing of football, as we saw with other schools in this section. The children's opinions were further consulted about other types of games which could be played in the play area. This resulted in the marking out of certain games in the play areas. It also had an effect upon the teaching of games in Physical Education lessons. New games were learned by the children, who had become interested in games. Old skills were also practised. The main problem associated with play — the playing of football — had to be resolved. It was given its place and each year group allocated one day to play. That prevented the older pupils from dominating all of every play time. If pupils are stimulated to play then they are less likely to indulge in bullying. The success of this approach can be judged by simply administering the playground survey again at some future time.

A further benefit to the school has been the interest shown by a local builder, following a teacher's placement in industry. The school's efforts in making the environment a more stimulating place had been discussed with the firm, who were only too willing to associate themselves with such positive moves and help the school. The firm's architect sketched out plans for an adventure playground, which the school has taken seriously. Obviously this is expensive but it can act as a focus for the community, encouraging involvement in all fund-raising activities. The firm was prepared to offset some of the costs even at the initial stages.

Finally an in-service day was organised for adults closely connected with the school, including all non-teaching staff and all the governors. This group of people drew the intertwining threads of the separate statements together in order to develop a whole school approach that included the behaviour and curricular policies. This represents an action plan and is symbolised by 'The Helping Hand' which summarises the drawing together of those separate threads.

The staff now feel that they have developed sufficient trust between themselves and the parents and children to allow the hidden behaviour — bullying — to be openly talked about. Importantly, the children and parents know it is safe to tell, that they will be listened to and that some action will be taken. Children now say in their own words, 'Telling about bullying is good'.

HELPING HAND

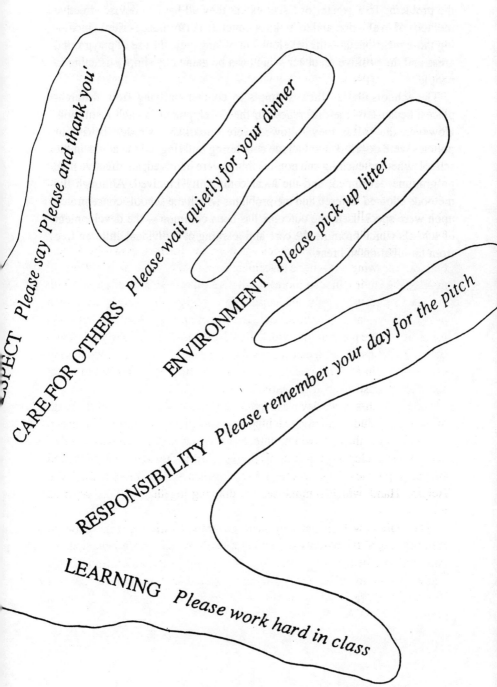

RESPECT Please say 'Please and thank you'

CARE FOR OTHERS Please wait quietly for your dinner

ENVIRONMENT Please pick up litter

RESPONSIBILITY Please remember your day for the pitch

LEARNING Please work hard in class

Comments

The programme to stop bullying in all of these schools is a rolling one. The staff do not think that they have now completed their work and eliminated the problem. To a greater or lesser extent they all have to devise effective methods of evaluation and to look for concrete performance criteria including those mentioned — the development of language, the use of playground areas and the positive feedback which can be gained by simply listening to people.

The schools started their attempts to counter bullying from different places, because of the differences in the development in each institution. However, the routes they followed were remarkably similar: behaviour policies were developed to include countering bullying; all the adults in the school, whether teaching and non-teaching, were involved; an effective PSE programme developed; and the local community involved. Although the methods adopted differed and the problems which the schools concentrated upon were specialised, the outcome has been common— the development of schools which promote the care and learning of individual children free from humiliation and fear.

4. Wycliffe College, Stonehouse, Gloucestershire

Allan Mason, Head of PSE

Wycliffe College is an independent, co-educational school, set in the heart of the Cotswolds. It is divided into two parts: the Junior School, with about 270 pupils (including the pre-prep department) taking children from 4-13 years old, and the Senior School of about 350 pupils taking girls and boys from ages 13-18.

The School was founded by GW Sibly in 1882, and has grown and developed since. It became a Public School in 1931 with a distinctive character, which remains today. The school grounds cover more than sixty acres and boast a wide range of modern facilities for providing relevant educational opportunities in a rapidly changing world.

The objectives of the school are:

- to provide the best possible academic training
- the belief that the training and development of the body as well as the mind is vital
- that we must also make young people aware of how to live and work with others
- to set targets for character building, leadership training and self motivation
- to recognise the importance of the spiritual elements of personal development.

Pupils are drawn from a wide variety of cultural and social backgrounds, an increasing number from overseas although most boarders live within an hour's drive of the school. The Midlands, London and South Wales are the main catchment areas for boarders; one third of pupils are day pupils and forty pupils are on the Assisted Places Scheme.

The school is organised on a House basis: five boarding houses (three for boys, two for girls) and one co-educational day pupil house. Each house accommodates from thirty to sixty pupils aged 13 to 18 years old, each with a resident housemaster or housemistress and family. Because of its size, Wycliffe is a very real community, and there is a natural friendliness built on the foundations of sensible discipline. Co-education enables the sexes to develop natural and relaxed friendships in a structured environment. Each pupil has a tutor, which increases the individuality of the pastoral care. In the first two years the pupil has a form tutor but in the following year chooses a member of staff to be his or her personal tutor for the remaining years at the school. This ensures greater respect and response than might be achieved by impersonal allocation. One of the strengths of the tutorial system and house system is that each pupil has two or more members of staff equally concerned to establish and encourage his or her integration into as many aspects of life in the school and the broader community as possible.

In April 1991 Wycliffe College was invited to send a representative (the Head of PSE) to attend a one day conference, 'Bullying — A Positive Response', organised by Gloucestershire Police Community Service Department as part of their 'National Crime Prevention Week' Campaign. The principal speaker at the conference was Delwyn Tattum. The initiative coincided with media attention on bullying in national papers and on radio and television.

Although the issue of bullying has always been treated seriously and sensitively in Wycliffe, the school did not have a specific policy. A decision was made to raise awareness among staff, pupils, governors and parents. This decision was not taken lightly as reservations were expressed about drawing attention to an issue which could be perceived by some parents and prospective parents as meaning that the school had a bullying problem.

A working group was set up in May 1991 with a brief to outline a draft policy statement. It consisted of the Head of PSE, an ex-housemaster of twelve years experience, a housemaster of a co-educational day pupil house, the Chaplain, to give a perspective outside Wycliffe, a female Year 9 tutor, and an assistant housemistress attached to a girls' boarding house, who is also a 6th form tutor.

The stages in the development of a strategy to counter and reduce bullying were identified as follows:

1. Research the extent of bullying through a school questionnaire
2. Analyse findings
3. Publish findings to staff
4. Develop a draft discussion document on the 'Whole School Policy'.
5. STAFF INSET — 'Bullying'
6. Publicise the agreed policy statement to staff, pupils, parents and governors
7. Prepare support material for: victims, bullies, staff, parents
8. Identify areas of responsibility for action and implementation of work with victim, bully and parents.

In July 1991 Delwyn Tattum invited Wycliffe to participate in a bullying project funded by the Calouste Gulbenkian Foundation. By then the questionnaire had been formulated and answered by pupils. By November 1991 stages 1-5 were complete, stage 6 and 8 were finalised by the end of the academic year 1992 and stage 7 support material was progressing.

A questionnaire was devised by the working group and subsequently approved by the Senior Management Group. It was given to all pupils in the school via form tutors and personal tutors in June 1991. It was considered important that pupils should have a clear understanding of what is meant by bullying. The definition given by Tattum and Herbert in *Bullying: A Positive Response* was printed at the top of the questionnaire, the tutors well briefed beforehand and the pupils given the opportunity to clarify any points of misunderstanding. Pupils were not required to identify themselves and knew the research was for internal information and publication only. The responses were processed by an optical reader card which restricted pupils to one response to each question. A total of 273 pupils took part.

Confidentiality does not permit publication of the full questionnaire results but it confirmed that regular bullying had taken place in the academic year 1990-91 and in previous years restricted, however, to a small percentage of pupils, half the national average for schools; 76% stated they had never been bullied. The nature of the bullying tended to be verbal rather than physical and consisted of name-calling, teasing and taunting. There was very little evidence of racial or sexual bullying. Groups rather than individuals were responsible. Bullies were either the same age or older than victims and the ratio of boys to girls involved in bullying was 5:1. A significant percentage of pupils did not seek help from staff, parents or senior pupils, being more likely to seek the assistance of a friend. Mostly they remained silent. The action taken by most victims was to avoid being singled out; some attempted to reason with the bully.

Bullying was most likely in the school grounds, less so in dormitories or study bedrooms, and significantly less in House common rooms and other areas of the school. Very rarely did a pupil miss school, miss a lesson or give up possessions through bullying behaviour. A few pupils admitted to doing something they did not want to do through peer pressure.

The Elton Report (1989) recommends that any school action to reduce bullying should be based on clear rules, appropriate sanctions and systems to support victims. It is recognised in Wycliffe that bullying is a complex problem and that what is perceived by one person to be bullying is perceived as boisterous or normal behaviour by another. The school is under no illusion about the long-term effects and unhappiness that can result from bullying, particularly where pupils cannot return to the safety and seclusion of a home environment. Parents place children in our charge confident in the knowledge that Wycliffe is as caring and secure as their home. As a boarding school, albeit with an increasing number of day pupils, the daily routine, supervision and care of pupils is significantly different from those of a maintained day school. The day is longer, 7.30am to 11.00pm for senior boarders, 8.30am to 6.45pm minimum for day pupils. It is not possible or desirable to police all areas of the school all the time, so efforts to reduce bullying must be through a programme of education and the creation of the right environment and ethos.

The House structure encourages competition in games, music and drama. House and team groups create an identity which is considered to be important; where there are groups it is inevitable that some pupils are excluded, thus creating conditions for bullying to take place. Maines and Robinson (1991) express concern that we expect too much when asking young people to discriminate between 'winning on the sports field through superior strength and using the same strategy to win power or possession in the playground. The language of success on the games field; 'I beat him...' I thrashed him...' is punished if it refers to a fight.' Developing a school ethos where bullying will not be tolerated, where bullies will be punished and victims protected is not enough. It is not 'helpful to regard bullying as absurd or evil.' However, it is the intent at Wycliffe to state that bullying is not an acceptable part of school life and we believe that all pupils have a basic right to receive their education free from humiliation and abuse whether physical or verbal. It is the interaction between an ordered school structure and the promotion and development of personal and social values such as empathy, consideration and unselfishness among pupils and staff which will help to change bullying behaviour. A policy based solely on prohibitions will not bring about lasting change.

In order to give effect to this philosophy the College has adopted a programme involving the following elements:

- An open and effective pastoral system
- An environment within the College not conducive to bullying
- The involvement of all teaching and support staff in the discussion and implementation of the policy
- A published and agreed procedure for dealing with bullying
- Advice for parents.

The structure of the pastoral system has already been outlined, involving house staff, year heads, tutors and medical staff. The weekly pastoral staff meeting is the key link in communication concerning pastoral matters. All staff attend and the meeting provides the forum for exchange of information and debate on individual pupils whose names have been recorded for discussion earlier in the week. If there is cause for concern, personal, social or academic, then immediate action can be taken by the relevant member of staff.

In making provision for an environment which is not conducive to bullying, the daily programme attempts to provide the right balance between work, recreation and rest. House staff are responsible for their own house environments and are very sensitive to the needs of the individual when placing pupils in dormitories and other shared accommodation.

Senior pupils have an important role to play both in houses and in the main school. To exercise their responsibilities effectively, it is recognised that they need training in leadership and personal skills. At the end of Year 12, all members of the year group who wish to be involved participate in a Sixth Form Responsibility Course. The day is led by a member of staff with wide experience in international training. House staff engage groups in role-play, discussion etc., exploring issues such as motivating others, making decisions and communication, with particular emphasis on responsibility and example-setting for younger pupils. At the beginning of Year 13 a similar course is run for prefects and further explores these ideas and concentrates on team building.

The Wycliffe day is supervised by a duty member of staff and three prefects or monitors. Checks are made on possible trouble spots outside the Houses and those areas of the school which are not constantly under direct supervision but are used by pupils in their free time eg. the Music School, CDT and Art Centre, squash courts, games and recreation areas and the town centre. All staff are aware of their responsibilities in terms of classroom professionalism and all that entails, ensuring that the school policy is in effective operation.

The campus is a large one so there is little overcrowding and a five minute change-over period between lessons gives pupils and staff opportunity to arrive on time for lessons. Specialised teaching blocks avoid the overcrowding typical of many main site buildings with narrow corridors and doorways. Meals are taken in four house dining rooms on a cafeteria basis. House staff and teaching staff also take their meals in these areas. Consequently, the standard of supervision is high and no pupil can be deprived of food. In this independent HMC, school pupils are well supplied with materials and textbooks so do not need to share, which is a known trigger for bullying behaviour.

The Education Reform Act states that the curriculum should promote the spiritual, moral, cultural, mental and physical development of pupils. Some of the underlying aims in the programme of personal and social education in Wycliffe, either through timetabled periods of PSE or more generally across the curriculum, are to encourage pupils to develop mutual respect and support, be aware and care for others, talk about feelings, be sensitive to the feelings of others and be responsible for their own behaviour. The climate in which PSE is taught encourages respect and mutual esteem. The involvement of pupils in group work and interaction encourages social confidence and co- operation. It is recognised that bullies tend to be assertive, to enjoy aggressive situations and be associated with anti-social behaviour and rule-breaking and that a high proportion are low achievers. Victims are often anxious and insecure, cautious, sensitive, lacking in self-confidence and have a poor self-esteem. The PSE programme addresses these issues at all stages of a pupil's development. A variety of teaching and learning methods are used and topics such as sanctions and rules, assertiveness, raising self-esteem, leadership, friendship, tolerance, values, peer pressure etc., are all designed to change attitudes, to develop a sense of responsibility, an awareness of the needs of others, an appreciation of individual differences and an appreciation of what others can offer.

In order to improve self-esteem and encourage constructive behaviour, staff are encouraged to react positively to pupils whenever possible. Achievements and effort are recognised in a variety of ways: positive report writing, Headmaster's commendation, prizes, colours, cups and ties awarded for contribution, achievement and kindness to others.

In November 1991, a Staff Discussion evening on 'Bullying' was held. Delwyn Tattum kindly agreed to be the speaker for the evening and chaired the discussion following his presentation. The purpose of this evening was to initiate a staff discussion on the development of a strategy to counter and reduce bullying in Wycliffe and to endorse the work already done. The evening was successful in giving bullying a high profile but probably raised as many questions as it answered.

However, despite the emphasis on developing self-esteem and good behaviour, which is the main preventative thrust of the response to counter bullying, there has to be an element of policing and sanctions for bad behaviour. On the occasions when bullying does take place, the agreed procedure for dealing with bullies and victims is implemented.

In December 1991 when the whole school policy on bullying was being developed, another working group in the school was engaged in implementing the Children Act 1989, Section 87. It soon became evident that there was a commonality of philosophy and procedure. The promotion of health, happiness and proper physical, emotional, social and behavioural developments and the protection against suffering, significant harm and neglect were key issues. Record keeping to ensure relevant information about individual children to inform decisions and serve as a record could apply equally to incidents of bullying. The regulations governing accommodation would further help to prevent bullying in residential areas of the school. With a common approach to rewards as well as sanctions, the complaints procedure could also be used for bullying complaints.

In January 1992 the Complaints Procedure was formulated by the Senior Mistress. It was approved and adopted by the staff after discussion during an INSET on the Children Act. This procedure was written and made available to staff, governors and parents. A more pupil friendly question and answer document is available for pupil use and guidance and is presented to pupils through tutors in PSE lessons. Helpline telephone numbers are also published in Houses.

Normally, it is hoped that if difficulties arise in the relationships between pupils, they will be dealt with informally by House staff, tutors, Chaplain or other members of staff as appropriate. In some situations, eg. serious bullying, there must be a more formal procedure of which staff and pupils are aware. In such situations pupils or parents may approach any member of staff— whoever they feel most comfortable with. It is expected that the member of staff nominated by the pupil should accompany him or her throughout the process, in a supporting role. Guidelines for 'Investigating a Case of Bullying', based on Besag (1989) is available to all staff.

It is considered important to take an account from the victim and really listen and note down the feelings expressed. This is followed by a meeting of those involved in the bullying; both the bullies and any passive onlookers. The problem is explained and the distress of the victim described. An attempt is made to get the group to identify strategies for dealing with the problem. The message must be conveyed that the bullies have reasons for what they do but they are misguided, have put themselves in the wrong and are capable of better behaviour. Another future meeting is arranged to monitor progress. If the seriousness of the incident warrants it, parents may be invited to withdraw the pupil from school for a period of time.

The programme of development is still continuing and amendments to the next edition of the School Rules will include a statement on bullying. The rules are published at the beginning of each academic year and a copy given to every pupil. It is also intended to make a statement on the school's bullying policy in the next revised edition of the prospectus. Present and prospective parents will be able to request a copy of this policy if they so wish.

No case of bullying is ever straighforward: in the very few instances when a pupil has been reported, invariably to the House staff, for bullying behaviour, the guidelines for dealing with a case have been followed. The incident has always been recorded but one Housemaster chose to communicate with parents by telephone rather than in writing as in the best interests of all concerned. The cases have been ones of verbal unpleasantness, teasing and the borrowing or hiding of possessions. There has been one case of physical violence where a fight between two pupils developed but this was not considered to be a bullying incident. All cases, which have involved both sexes, have been dealt with successfully and the positive relationships between the pupils restored.

5. Eastbourne Comprehensive School, Darlington
Bob Dingle, Headteacher
Barbara Thompson, Deputy Headteacher
Dudley Wright, Deputy Headteacher

Eastbourne Comprehensive School was established in 1968 when Eastbourne Secondary Modern Boys' School was amalgamated with the Girls' School. The architecture is substantial, pleasant and remodelled buildings of the inter-war years. The school caters for pupils aged 11 to 16; those continuing in full time education move on to the local sixth form college or the college of technology. The premises stand in 30 acres of grounds and offer good facilities for both academic and supporting activities. There are 800 pupils on roll.

The school serves the immediate community, of mainly council-owned houses with a sprinkling of privately owned housing. The area suffers from a high level of unemployment and economic depression, indicated by the large number of pupils who are entitled to free meals — about 30%. The socio/economic background mitigates against positive relationships between pupils and their teachers, since most pupils and their parents have low expectations of academic success. A significant proportion of the pupils have poor self-esteem and lack the skills necessary to make the most of their school life.

5.1 The beginnings
A radical shake-up of the school's management structures enabled an energised staff to consider, during an INSET session, which statements best represented the collective view of the values and practices which could ideally form the basis of life at the school. These statements were articulated into a 'Vision for Eastbourne School', which summarised the views of the staff about the aims and objectives of school life and the ways in which they might be implemented. What follows is a summary of those statements and an expression of the philosophy of the school.

School experiences should be enjoyable for all concerned. Pupils should be encouraged to assume as much responsibility as is practicable for every aspect of their membership of school. This includes: appearance, behaviour, the quality of relationships and participation with regard to the curriculum. The same applies equally to staff. The principles of involvement and participation lead to ownership and commitment.

The formal rules of the school must be as few and as simple as possible, dealing solely with the education, safety and happiness of the pupils, staff and the community. Areas of possible conflict are recognised and must be approached jointly by pupils and staff. As a basic principle, all aspects of violence should be discouraged in all interactions between school members.

Equality of opportunity within the curriculum should be proactively pursued, addressing issues arising from gender, colour and race, creed, social class and special educational needs. The principal task for the school is the provision of a curriculum for all its members. To achieve this, a holistic approach is necessary and should include important elements of the hidden curriculum: the physical appearance of the school, the appearance and the conduct of relationships between staff and pupils, the opportunities afforded to pupils for choice of curriculum, and the development of the pupils' role in school. The delivery of the curriculum should be based upon these principles as well as those set out in the National Curriculum and should adapt to accommodate both, including easing the transition from feeder schools and promoting continuity.

To increase their understanding of the curriculum, it was proposed to invite all governors to the separate planning meetings to participate and help in reaching decisions. Parents were also welcomed to visit the school, although it is recognised that this is more problematic than inviting governors.

5.2 Further development

Having reached this consensus with the staff, it became clear that the quality of life for both staff and pupils would be much improved if an initiative to counter bullying was begun. The staff agreed that it was something which could be profitably addressed and complimented the statements summarised above. At the same time the LEA, quite independently of the school, began an initiative to develop a county-wide policy. On hearing of the school's initiatives, it offered one of its representatives to become part of the working party in the school.

Developments proceeded in a number of ways. The interpersonal skills required to implement the ideas were so great that not everything could be planned for. However, a framework could be set up that would stimulate individual members of staff into ownership of the steps forward.

The first stage required staff to recognise the problem of bullying, which affected all pupils in school. Pastoral staff and the Senior Management Team were aware that the problem existed, but how widespread it was had not been quantified. In order to give the initiative the required status, it was written into the school management plan and a programme was carefully costed. This plan allowed for INSET for five senior staff to write guidelines for the rest of the staff. Heads of Year discussed these guidelines within their year teams so that every member of staff was consulted. Year teams addressed the problem of bullying in their PSE programmes. A sensitively worded letter was sent to parents explaining why the school was focusing its attentions on bullying and asking for their help in the process. Senior staff addressed the problem of bullying in all year and school assemblies, as well as explaining the school's policy and how it affected the pupils, so as to show a commitment to pupils and staff.

There was an immediate increase in the number of referrals, as most schools have noted. Establishing the climate of a 'telling' school is an important process in the moves to combat bullying and is underlined by the increase in the number of referrals.

In the curriculum, all Year 9 pupils addressed bullying as an issue in the Key Stage 3 pilot SAT for English. Stimuli came from a variety of sources: poems, videos, literature, newspapers, tapes and so on. A number of interesting articles were written by the pupils, following the initiative taken in the curriculum. This poem was written by a Year 9 pupil:

The Bully

I like to watch you cry. Although
I wouldn't want you to die. I also
like to see you squirm, just like
a dying worm
When I walk down the corridor
all the kids run a mile or more.
I make fun of their clothes and I
know all the time it's me they
loathe.
How many kids have I beaten up?
And felt their anger building up?
How many kids have I punched
in the face? Or made fun of at
the school gate?
I'm getting sick of this bullying
lark. Some people think it's a
proper laugh.
Now I think it's a real waste. I
don't know why I started in the
first place.

Year 9 pupil

5.3 Evaluation

After an initial review of the progress of the work, it was decided to plan a questionnaire which would give some quantifiable data. This could then be used as an initial audit for future comparisons to be made. The pastoral staff have drawn up a further action plan which is to be implemented over the coming years. This includes INSET monies devoted to the training of midday supervisors. The drawing up of that action plan has also lead to a summary of the school's work to date, which is set out as follows:

- ■ Initially it was important to raise awareness amongst all staff and pupils. No assumptions about behaviour could be made.

- ■ School guidelines were drawn up to help with actions which teachers could take. They also offered help to the victim, the bully, parents and governors.

- ■ Claims about bullying were taken seriously at all times. The problem was dealt with immediately and not put off until some future time. Victims were protected and the plan of action explained to them.

- ■ Even if the staff felt that a pupil was making much of a minor incident, to the pupil it was real and was treated accordingly — at least until investigations were made.

- ■ The major performance indicator used by the school was to make the school a 'telling school'. By dealing with an increased number of referrals, the staff felt it was becoming more effective in countering bullying, since parents and their children trusted the school and its systems.

6. St. Mary's C. of E. Primary School, Manchester

Emyr Roberts, Headteacher

The school is a one stream entry primary school, catering for pupils age 4 to 11. There are 370 pupils on roll. The school was built in 1971 — a one storey building set in pleasant parkland. The school has a socially mixed catchment area, drawing equally from privately owned and council owned housing. The school has aided status and has close connections with St Mary's Church of England Church which is situated some fifty yards from the school.

6.1 The beginnings

The initiative began out of the Governors' need to draw up a discipline policy for the school, as statutorily required. This coincided with a growing concern amongst the entire school population that bullying incidents seemed to be increasing during the school day. Both the teaching staff and the Governing Body became increasingly involved in discussions and workshops to draw up the discipline policy for the school. They relied heavily on the recommendations of the Elton Report (1989), the Local Education Authority's guidelines and the advice given in *Bullying: A Positive Response*.

The teaching staff decided to look at the specific problem of bullying in some detail. First they drew up a list of where the reported incidents of bullying were happening. They discovered that few incidents of bullying were brought to their notice during classroom lessons, although they recognised that verbal taunts could occur without the knowledge of the staff. However well organised a modern classroom is, there is always the opportunity for a bully to frighten weaker pupils.

The staff wished to bring the issue into the open and discussed a variety of strategies for doing so. This included the pupils producing posters for display around the school; providing pupils with the stimulus for creative writing about bullying and the ways they could think of countering the problem; the use of drama and role play. The emphasis was on self-help and pupils were encouraged to discuss their experiences in general terms and how they could help each other. The pupils were comforted by the fact that the staff had begun to take the problem seriously, were sympathetic and were ready and willing to act against any instances of verbal abuse. The personal and social development of the bullies were also considered and strategies designed for counselling bullies.

6.2 Initial developments

Teachers and pupils discussed where and when bullying most commonly occurred. Through discussion, two main times were identified:

1. during the mass movement in and out of school
    at the beginning of the school day;
    at the break and dinner time;
    at the end of the school day.
2. During the lunch break.

Next, the staff identified the danger points of movement in and out of school where intimidation could occur, and the whole procedure for these movements was reviewed. The suggested new procedures were discussed with the pupils before being implemented and their opinions acted upon. The new procedures involved:

- Supervision of the pupils' use of the cloakroom areas
- Monitoring the use of the toilets
- Staggering of dismissals from classrooms.

Implementing the pupils' opinions made them feel that they were being taken seriously. It produced a greater commitment on the pupils' part to following the procedures and increased the pupils' confidence in the staff's ability to counter bullying.

However, most bullying took place during the lunch break. In discussions with the school's staff and pupils this was attributed to three main causes:

1. The lunch break was long. Many pupils became bored and looked for mischief to relieve that boredom. Consequently the lunch break was shortened.
2. The school yard had little to offer the pupils. It was an unstimulating environment and this too led to boredom. This was discussed with the lunchtime organisers and the pupils. A variety of games were then supplied by the school, involving areas for skipping; boxes of balls to play with; drawing circles on walls and ground to help formation of games; drawing hopscotch lines ; organising ring games.
3. The main reason, however, was considered to be the low status of the lunchtime organisers within the school structure. Despite this, it was they who had the most difficult supervisory roles. They could not become too involved in the organising of games for the pupils, since they had to maintain an overall view of the yard. Furthermore, their lack of status in the pupils' eyes made it difficult for them to intervene in any meaningful way in the pupils' social development and relationships.

WHAT'S SO GOOD ABOUT BEING A LUNCHTIME ORGANISER?

<u>You said........</u>

Keeping children safe and happy at lunchtime.

Playing games with youngsters.

Being part of a team.

Knowing that I'm a valuable member of the community.

Some children don't get shown much love at home. I
can make sure they get some at school.

When you teach children games, you know you are
passing on lasting traditions.

The conversation and company of children.

LUNCHTIME ORGANISER

MANCHESTER CITY COUNCIL JOB DESCRIPTION

Lunchtime Organiser

Main Purpose of the Job

Supervision of the pupils in the dining area/s and elsewhere as required by the Headteacher.

Main Tasks

1) To communicate with the pupils in their care
2) To supervise pupils in the dining area/s and elsewhere as required by the Headteacher
3) To help create an atmosphere so that the meal and lunchtime recreation is a pleasant experience for pupils and staff
4) Taking pupils who have minor accidents or are unwell to the Senior Lunchtime Organiser, for first-aid where necessary, if first aid is not necessary comforting and re-assuring them.
5) To report more serious accidents to the Senior Lunchtime Organiser.
6) To accompany sick or injured pupils home or to hospital, in a taxi or other transport provided.
7) Where the need arises for instance with young children, or children with special needs attending to their physical needs such as handwashing, feeding and toileting.

"The postholder must carry his/her duties with full regard to the Council's Equal Opportunities Policy.

The Education Committee believes that the Education Service should be founded on equal rights, equal opportunities, mutual respect and social justice. All employees are expected to behave in a way which values equally all members of the public, other employees, students and pupils regardless of race, ethnic or cultural group. Employees are also encouraged and will be supported to be critical of institutional practices and procedures that work against equal rights, equal opportunities, mutual respect and social justice.

Equal Opportunities In Education: Anti-Racist Policy Statement

SOME IMPORTANT POINTS ABOUT SANCTIONS

- You must feel happy with the Sanctions, or you will be tempted to let the children off.

- Everyone in the school should be informed of them. The children in particular need to be fully aware of the consequences of breaking a school rule.

- Parents should be informed.

- Sanctions should be applied consistently.

- They should be delivered in a calm manner (remember to criticize the behaviour, not the child).

- Wherever possible they should be delivered by the lunchtime organiser. However, it may be necessary also to inform the classteacher/headteacher.

Meetings of lunchtime organisers were held and their views invited and discussed. At first they were embarrassed about even being consulted, but their confidence soon grew and they began to contribute more readily. Their ideas proved to be practical and valid, and wherever possible their suggestions were implemented.

■ Unmarked zones were introduced into the Junior yard at lunch time to which pupils of different age groups and interests were confined. This ensured that the older boys in particular, who like to play football, did not dominate the entire yard. There were now places in the yard for the younger pupils and for those who wished to play at quieter games.

■ Flexibility was built into this system, to allow for inter-age friendships to continue or be developed. The school budget allowed for an increase in the number of lunchtime organisers and each one was allocated a specific zone within the yard for which the individual organiser was responsible. This enabled each one to come to know the pupils as individuals.

■ These initiatives and their purposes were discussed with the pupils, who responded in a positive and responsible way so that play at lunchtime was generally more peaceful and there was less disruption.

Perhaps the greatest benefit has been to raise the self-esteem of the lunchtime organisers. They feel that their views are respected and worth listening to, which results in greater commitment to their job.

Giving Praise

GOOD NEWS FROM SCHOOL

Dear Parent,
        I am writing
to tell you how pleased I
was with ___ behaviour
at lunchtime today. I
saw _____ which
was _____ and a good
example to the other
children.

                Yours Sincerely

GOOD NEWS FROM SCHOOL

GOOD NEWS FROM SCHOOL

GOOD NEWS FROM SCHOOL

All of this, however, did not eliminate the hard core of bullies in the school nor did it fully protect their unfortunate victims. The lunchtime organisers came up with the idea of giving pupils who required it the close attention of one particular organiser. Those pupils considered most vulnerable were allocated to their 'own' organiser, who gets to 'know' her pupil well and appreciate the fears the pupil experiences. Whenever individual pupils feel threatened they can approach the lunchtime organiser who will give immediate support. Depending on the urgency of the situation, the bully can be removed from the yard and dealt with at a convenient time by the Senior Lunchtime Organiser or the Headteacher. The emphasis is therefore on the protection of the victim and not immediately on the punishment of the bully.

Giving Praise — Happygram

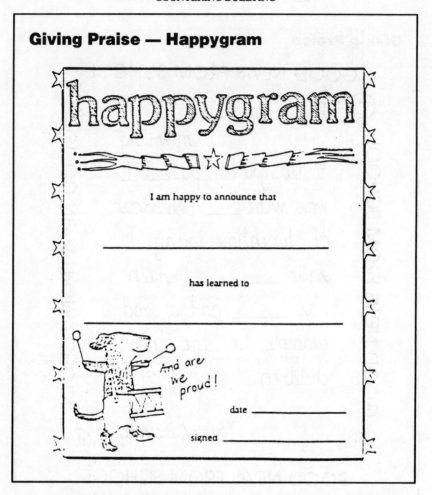

6.3 Further developments

The training of Lunchtime Organisers has been greatly aided by the Report of the Lunchtime Organisers Project by the North Manchester District Support Team. This has provided valuable information for schools to use with their lunchtime staff. The booklet is specifically aimed at helping these important members of school staff to fulfil their jobs, by raising their self-esteem, advising them about how to deal with problem behaviour and suggesting games for the children to play.

At the same time, the school became involved in a cluster project involving two High Schools and their twelve feeder schools which organised in-service training on the management of behaviour. The Headteachers and Deputies met on a regular basis and it was decided that the cluster would organise its own in-service which emphasised the importance of listening skills and conflict resolution. The group came up with specific proposals:

Recommendations

The group responded to the conference evaluation forms. Twenty forms were returned and the issues that people felt should be addressed were as follows:

1. The feeling that sharing and working together should be fostered within the cluster. That schools could be involved in joint projects, perhaps that two or three schools work jointly on areas of common concern. There should be an opportunity for Staffs to see good practice in other schools.

2. There should be a Cluster Group Policy for children with extreme behavioural difficulties.

3. There should be INSET provision within the Cluster and that should take several forms:

   a) regular weekend conferences
   b) regular twilight sessions

This should be planned annually within the Cluster.

4. Individual schools should look at their present practice, particularly in terms of in-school communication systems and present classroom practices. It was felt that a Whole School approach to organisation and planning was *vital*.

5. Lunchtime Organisers were an important part of a school's behaviour policy and should be involved in INSET activities. Schools needed guidance on LO training.

6. There should be Assertiveness Training for Staff and children.

7. There should be a session to give schools the opportunity to see the Lee Canter materials in greater detail.

8. Guidance to help schools build 'pastoral' issues into their School Development Plans.

9. There should be a submission to the LEA pressing the need for a well communicated and effective whole-city policy for disruptive children.

10. The cluster should work towards closer bonding with the High Schools.

11. There should be some form of Outreach work.

12. The question of why children are disruptive should be addressed.

13. How can the Cluster support the dissemination of conference material into schools.

14. Express the effect that the school's physical and emotional environment has on children.

15. There should be a series of meetings on awareness raising, personality clashes, teaching and learning styles. Stressing the importance of being positive, listening, confidence building and seeing things from the child's perspective.

These meetings gave all those involved the opportunity to work towards solutions to the common problems regarding behaviour. It proved far less stressful than working in isolation.

Comment

Countering bullying in each of these schools is ongoing. None of the schools feels it has succeeded in beating the problem. However, all can be justifiably proud of their attempts at minimising the problem as it affects their pupils. A similar pattern has emerged from these schools in that they see the role of effective management as the vital ingredient in combating bullying. Although the routes adopted by individual schools have varied according to a variety of factors — historical developments, staffing, school development priorities and so on — the outcomes have been common, namely, the creation of a school which promotes the care and learning of individual children free from humiliation and fear.

The first step has been to raise awareness, not only among the staff but also among the pupils, about the nature of bullying. Following this process, which can take a long time, wide-ranging consultation has taken place, so that all staff feel party to the forthcoming changes. The schools have drawn up a policy or set of guidelines, circulated for comment and amended if necessary. The pupils have also played a vital part in this process. The policy, or set of procedures, has been communicated to the rest of the community, using a variety of devices, from letters sent home to using the school brochure or handbook. In some cases the school's newsletter has been a useful medium. The procedures have been reviewed on a regular basis so that the impetus for change is not lost. Each school has looked also for effective performance criteria and these have varied according to both circumstances and the original aims of the programme.

Theme Two

Using the Curriculum

Introduction

In the previous theme, the approaches adopted by schools concentrated on the management of the initiatives. One of the important functions of management is to enable and oversee the delivery of the curriculum. However, schools are concerned with fostering the learning of not only relevant facts and concepts but also attitudes, values and beliefs. The ways in which these effective elements in the curriculum can have a positive effect upon the pupils and the environment in which they learn is outlined in this section. It is noticeable that the work in these schools is effective because much of the energy and many of the ideas come from the pupils themselves. Thus the pupils become part of the programme to improve their own learning environment while also caring for the well-being of their more vulnerable members. That the curricular initiative belongs to the pupils themselves, as do the outcomes of those initiatives, is a central theme in the approaches outlined in this section of the report. This procedure is totally different from the introduction of the National Curriculum, about which even the teachers had little say.

Following the description of the schools' developments, the editors contribute their own ideas to the debate. Little thought has been given to how the curriculum can be used as a tool for countering bullying effectively.

In fact the schools in this section, and perhaps in the entire report, are in the vanguard of such thinking.

If the management initiatives are to have any lasting effect, then they must be incorporated into the curriculum itself and its delivery. As La Fontaine (1991) points out, the bully acts in a certain way because the balance of power rests with him or her. If we are to shift that balance of power, we must convince pupils that we are serious about tackling a problem which affects *them* rather than the staff. To achieve this we must look beyond the short-term measures adopted to counter bullying and look towards the medium and long-term. This is most effectively achieved by incorporating into the delivery of the curriculum itself an anti-bullying element.

Although the National Curriculum must be delivered, it can be done in imaginative and stimulating ways. This does not simply mean using PSE as a means of countering bullying through the curriculum, although this is a valid option. As has been argued elsewhere: 'The fear and misery does not disappear with the end of tutorial time, but is carried on into Maths or Science or Games' (Herbert 1988). As the following examples show, a wealth of ideas is available which will shift the balance of power away from the bully.

St John Wall R.C. Comprehensive School began their initiatives through English and Drama; it soon developed into other areas, notably the delivery of PSE. In this area, the pupils contributed effectively to the delivery, by writing their own materials. The work spread through Technology and even into extra-curricular work.

Malvern Girls' College took up the theme in their delivery of Religious Education. This too spread into other areas, notably the pastoral structure and the care given to the girls. The perceptiveness of the complex social situations which lead to bullying is quite evident here and shows the levels of understanding of which all our pupils are capable.

The staff at Pensby High School for Boys tackled the issue on a number of fronts, supporting Askew's (1988) views that bullying in an all-boys school can become institutionalised, reflecting and reinforcing stereotypical views of masculinity. The ethos of the school was such that it could ask pertinent questions of itself quite openly. That these processes led to a serious look at curricular provision strengthens the view that the curriculum can be a tool for the countering of bullying, or a vehicle allowing for its perpetuation.

1. St John Wall R.C. Comprehensive School, Birmingham

Jean Whitney, Teacher of English and Drama

This school is a Roman Catholic comprehensive catering for pupils age 12 to 16. It is situated some three miles from Birmingham City centre in Handsworth. It is a popular, over-subscribed school with a five form entry and numbers rising towards 600. It is thought to be unique since it is a 'Catholic' school which caters for children of varied ethnic origin and religious belief. There are children whose parents hail from India, Pakistan, Vietnam, China, the Caribbean, Africa, Eire and Britain. This diversity creates a rich cultural mix which thrives in the caring, Catholic ethos of the school.

A spell to make a bully into a nice person
First a dose of weakness to take away your strength;
Then a dose of softener to soften up your voice.
Now I'll try some tenderness to take away your punch;
Now some muscle relaxer to ease away your kick.
Then I'll try a dose of respect to teach you some manners.
Finally an extra large dose of love to take away the pain
Within your heart, and give you a warm and loving nature.'
Marcus Patterson

This spell was written by a Year 8 boy in response to the anti-bullying programme which begins very early in the pupils' secondary school career. It illustrates the message which the school tries to convey: bullies themselves need help, first to realise what they are doing to others and then to correct their behaviour.

1.1 Beginnings

The initiative began some time ago when a number of elements came together: a senior member of staff had attended a course on the topic; the topic was being addressed in an English class with year 8 pupils; the Big Brum Theatre Company was invited into school to perform 'The Killing Ground' to Year 8 pupils. Around this time, the booklet *Bullying: A Positive Response* (1990) arrived in school. Its usefulness was immediately recognised and further copies were bought for each department to use.

The programme began to take shape, slowly at first. Year 9 pupils were asked to look at the topic of bullying from the point of view of both bully and victim. It was recognised that, given different circumstances, this could be one and the same person. Much lively discussion took place, together with some drama presenting scenes which involved bullying situations. Strategies were discussed for dealing with each situation. The culmination of working with this particular group was the production of a booklet 'Bullying — Who Needs It?' which contains children's poems and suggestion for follow on work.

The children's booklet was used as the basis for an assembly in which pupils read some of their poems and talked about how they came to write them. The assembly was well received by the rest of the school and awareness of the topic had been raised. A set of similar booklets was produced and these are now used as part of the Year 7 PSE programme. The pupils involved were proud of their contribution to the curriculum. The presentation of the booklet involved English, Drama and Technology, through the use of the word processor, and proved a useful and stimulating exercise. Many of the pupils mentioned it as an addition to their Record of Achievement. On page 65 and 66 two poems from the booklet are presented, together with the suggested follow-up work.

The Big Brum Theatre Company's production of 'The Killing Ground' traced the causes of a young girl's suicide back through bullying experiences at work, at home and at school. The workshops following the performance involved the pupils acting out similar situations to the ones presented and was followed by suggestions about how situations could have been improved and behaviour modified. The fact that bullying was not confined to children in school was highlighted and much valuable drama written work ensued.

1.2 Further developments

From these beginnings the anti-bullying programme has developed. It is now a recognised part of the curriculum with a concentration on Year 7 to reassure the incoming pupils and to set the tone for the remainder of their time in the school. A module has been devised for the lower school which invites discussion of many aspects of bullying and makes use of materials in *English at Nelson Street* (1988), the above-mentioned booklet and the pupils' own booklet.

The anti-bullying programme in Year 7 is delivered in PSE as well as other areas of the curriculum. This occupies one period per week plus some registration or tutorial time. This is primarily a skills course aimed at improving self-confidence through a variety of different units.

The school has tried to link PSE, English, Drama, IT and RE in work on anti-bullying themes. A recent TVEI funded initiative involved the head of English introducing newly-arrived Year 7 pupils to a group of Year 10 pupils

KICK HIM IN!

I walked around the corner,
I saw him,
I had to do something
Or I would have been thought of
as a softy.
All my friends started on me.
'Go on! Now's your chance!'
'Kick him in!'

I went over to him.
He saw me.
He knew I was going to do
something
So he turned and walked away
from me.
I could see him shivering
But it wasn't really that cold.
I couldn't think of what to do to
him
Against the wall.
'Give me all your money!'
'No,' he said,
Dropping his bag.
I punched him in the stomach.
I looked at the boys, smiling.
They were pleased.
Pick up his bag!'
'Throw it!' they said.

I picked it up.
I told him to give me his money
Or I would throw his bag away
Into the grotty bin.
'All right, all right,' he said.
He gave me his money, crying.

But, still being watched by the
boys,
I threw his bag anyway.

Then I ran back.
The boys congratulated me;
Slapped me on the back and all
that.
I felt good,
But deep inside,
I knew it was
Wrong.

Jatinder Dhillon

DISCUSSION POINTS

'Kick Him In'

What kind of boy is the 'bully' in this poem?
What effect do his friends have on the situation?
Would he act this way if he was alone?
Does the boy feel comfortable about his own behaviour?
Can you imagine why the boy needs to go to such
lengths to please his friends?
Write a few lines of advice to this boy (in the form of a
poem if you can) which might enable him to change his
ways.

VICTIM

I have to go to school tomorrow
I know what to expect.
My teachers don't listen,
My parents just say,
'Fight back!'
But I'm not the type to fight
Back again and again and again
I'm sad to think of school and
Happy to feel safe at home.
Sometimes I don't want to go so
I make an excuse to my mum
And dad.

I feel trapped inside the school
And someone else is in control
Of my life.

Why should I put up with this
And the other
Because I'll get battered or
Cussed in front of my friends?
If it happens again I'll kill
Myself

As I can't face it any more.
At least the shame and pain
Will be over
Once and for
All.

Rajinder Pal

DISCUSSION POINTS

'Victim'

This victim feels 'trapped' inside this situation. Can you explain why trapped is such a suitable word to use?

He says, 'My teachers don't listen.' Can you suggest ways in which you can gain a teacher's attention if you have something worrying you?

His parents say, 'Fight back!' Imagine you are the boy's father or mother — write a short poem in which you advise your son on how to deal with the bullies.

as part of the latter's GCSE coursework. This was done by means of the older pupils writing letters to the incoming pupils from the junior school, welcoming them, asking them what their fears and concerns were on joining the 'big' school and assuring them that it was possible to survive! The year 7 pupils were delighted to receive this correspondence and pleased to form a link with a senior pupil. Their replies revealed that one of their fears was the possibility of being bullied by older pupils — a message which struck a chord in their hosts in year 10. Meetings were arranged between the pupils and some were recorded on video to be used as part of the pupils' GCSE oral work. This type of activity cannot help but create a caring atmosphere.

Another project in Drama uses puppets. A 'Punch and Judy' script is available which has Mr Punch involved in wife-beating, and generally bullying all and sundry. Although we have used Mr Punch to entertain children for years, it is more fun for children to see the tables turned on this rogue. Large puppets have also been developed to act out some sensitive situations which occur in school. Pupils are able to relate to the puppets, when open discussion of a similar situation may prove too difficult.

The parents, governors and local community are all involved in the cultivation of a 'caring' ethos which creates a non-threatening atmosphere for the pupils in school. The school is situated on a small estate of elderly people's homes. The residents are often invited into the school for entertainments and parties after school. Many of them are visited by the pupils and a friendly association prevails. Parents or guardians are invited to become 'Friends of St John Wall', as well as parent governors. They are made aware of the policies and asked to support the school in its efforts to provide a safe environment for the pupils. The parents or guardians of pupils who admit to being bullies are invited into school for discussion about possible strategies to help the child. Persistent offenders, together with their parents or guardians, are brought before the Governing Body. A contract is drawn up, outlining the terms under which the child will be allowed to remain at the school. If the contract is broken the parents may be asked to find another school for their child. Bullying is a serious offence and is treated as such.

RE occupies an important place in the school's curriculum. Themes of caring, kindness, social justice and so on are given a high profile. A voluntary Mass is held in the chapel every Friday, although many pupils attend. The School Chaplain is a well known figure and offers a sympathetic and confidential ear.

To support this service, the School Nurse holds a fortnightly 'drop in' session when pupils may call in to discuss any topic that is of concern to them. These sessions are a recent development. The times are advertised on posters displayed prominently in the school. Response to them has been encouraging. The Nurse offers confidentiality and will only divulge information to staff with the pupil's permission. The need for confidentiality is crucial to this kind of support. Pupils have expressed doubts about queuing to see the nurse, since they claim it creates an opportunity for the vulnerable to be teased further. The mid-day supervisors and caretaking staff also have their parts to play in countering bullying. Their vigilance is also requested and they are made aware of the systems to adopt if they encounter such behaviour.

1.3 Conclusion

Opening up the dark corners of the world of the bully has been a stimulation to the whole of the affective curriculum. Making pupils and staff aware that bullying will not be tolerated is an on-going process. Pupils need to feel that they can speak out without feeling that they are 'grassing'. Although the problem is not beaten, it is constantly tackled. Pupils are more ready to talk about the problem and to report incidents, whether these affect them or others. It has been encouraging to hear other pupils intervene on behalf of one of their peers, or to hear someone admit that his teasing could be hurtful. Nevertheless the onus remains with the staff to create the atmosphere where such matters can be discussed and where vulnerable pupils are afforded confidentiality.

2. Malvern Girls' College
Reverend Pauline Newton, Deputy Headteacher

Another curricular approach was illustrated by a girls' independent school. Such a school has to face a number of problems with which schools in the state sector do no have to contend. Malvern Girls' College is a single-sex school of some 520 pupils of whom 450 are boarders and the rest day girls. The school has always prided itself on the pastoral care of the girls. Bullying had never been considered a major problem. This does not mean that no girl had difficulty in making friends or adjusting to the different demands of boarding, but they had found ways of coping, usually by talking to someone — friends, staff or parents — and the situation has not become too worrying. Very occasionally a serious problem has occurred and then staff have intervened and tough measures have been taken. It has been made clear to the bully that the school will not accept such behaviour. If her behaviour does not improve, the girl has been asked to leave.

2.1 The beginnings

The issue of bullying was taken up by the media on a number of occasions and staff felt it was a topic worth considering in a lifeskills lesson with Year 11 pupils. With form tutors, the pupils discussed various points which had been raised by their stimuli. To the staff's surprise, the girls felt strongly that some sort of policy should be developed to help pupils who might experience difficulties at the school. Although they agreed that most people would know to whom they could turn if they needed help or advice, they displayed commendable compassion for the minority for whom employing some sort of procedure would help. To harness this opinion amongst the girls it was decided to try to determine what the school as a whole felt about the issue of bullying. One form, with the guidance of their form tutor, prepared a questionnaire.

As is the case with many such questionnaires, the format was not as clear as it might have been and it raised almost as many questions as it sought to answer. Some of the answers were not straightforward yes or no replies and this created problems when collating the responses. To overcome the problems of interpretation it was decided to create a 'miscellaneous' response. There was no definition of bullying but the girls would have concurred with the views of La Fontaine (1991) when she explains that bullying occurs when the victim is caused emotional or physical pain. The intentions of the bully are secondary as the focus is on the victim's feelings.

The questionnaire was completed during tutorial time and the whole school took part. When the results had been analysed, the staff were left feeling concerned about the number of girls who said they had been bullied.

These results were then discussed with more year groups. It soon emerged that the staff's perception of the situation was a typical adult one and limited in scope. The girls accepted that the school dealt strongly with the few reported cases of bullying but that this was not the full picture. They considered that a wide range of activities could be called bullying and much of it would go unreported. However, though unreported, it did not mean that pain and suffering were not experienced. The questionnaire had made it clear that a procedure for dealing with all levels of bullying was called for.

As a way of raising the whole school's awareness, Year 11 pupils presented the results of the questionnaire to a school assembly and high-lighted their reports with sketches. They also announced that a procedure for dealing with bullying would be outlined in succeeding months. It was considered important that the initiative be announced by the pupils, since it was they who had instigated the staff's actions and they would at least have ownership of the programme. How could the staff proceed? Before decisions were taken, it was felt that much more information was needed.

2.2 Gathering information

The next move was to ask some of the year groups to write more extensively about bullying so that the staff could have an in-depth view of the nature of bullying as perceived by the pupils. The three lower years were considered the most vulnerable and thus targeted. The boarding school is divided into Middle School (Year 7-11) and Sixth Form Houses, so the oldest pupils in Middle Studies Department are Year 11 girls. With the support of the Religious Studies Department, time was devoted to the topic of bullying and the girls were asked the following questions:

- What should be done to help those being bullied?
- What should be done to help bullies?
- Please comment on anything else you feel would be helpful.

The girls wrote anonymous accounts and were open and honest. Although not asked to write about the sort of bullying individual people experienced, a few did mention that verbal comments such as criticism of clothes, hair style or physical features were as hurtful as physical forms of bullying.

Mental bullying is worse than physical, it destroys all self-confidence
(Year 9 girl)

However, there was some feeling that girls are also sensitive, cry easily and take things too much to heart. A few girls felt that the school was in danger of over-reacting.

People should learn to take criticism and a joke. They should learn to ignore nasty comments (Year 9 girl).

On the whole there was a real depth of understanding of the insidious nature of bullying and the effect it has on people.

I think they should comfort and support the victims and make them feel secure (Year 8 girl).

Some children who are bullied get scared and lose all their self-motivation and determination. You have to help them get it back and convince them what the bully said was wrong (Year 9 girl).

The understanding of the bully's position and what motivated her was also astute.

One case of bullying at my old school was because the girl concerned had just been told that her mother was going to have a baby. When the baby came, everyone was so thrilled with it they completely ignored the other girl. So she took out all her jealousy and rage on the other children who were small and weak, just like a baby (Year 8 girl).

The bully should be helped by kindness. If they are just punished it won't help them because they must have a problem at home or at school to make them bully people (Year 7 girl).

Bullies are often the ones who really need help. A lot of the time they are people who at some time have been discriminated against and therefore seem to want to get at people who are as insecure as themselves. They despise themselves and take it out on others (Year 9 girl).

One girl in year 8 gave 16 reasons why someone could resort to being a bully:

1. *Divorce of parents*

2. *Unhappiness in the family*

3. *Lost friendships*

4. *School work becoming too hard*

5. *A feeling of insecurity*

6. *Loneliness or isolation*

7. *A bad reputation*

8. *A distraction in the family causing one of the children to be ignored*

9. *Unhappiness*

10. *Jealousy*

11. *Someone bullying you so you bully someone else*

12. *Too much pressure on the person*

13. *GCSE or 'A' Levels*

14. *Failure to get on with a person in your family/House/School*

15. *Other people slagging you off*

16. *Malicious rumours*

Such perceptiveness is not uncommon. However, it can only come to light if the pupils are given the opportunity to write about the topic as part of their curricular provision. Left only to discussion, the lack of anonymity would restrict the revelation of such insights. It was clear from the girls' written comments that whilst most girls believed they could cope if they were bullied, they wanted a system for their weaker colleagues. The majority of the girls were adamant that they would tell someone quickly if they felt they had been bullied.

I would go to my sister or my Housemistress (Year 7 girl).

I think the best thing to do would be to tell a close friend first and discuss it with her... Then if the situation gets worse tell a member of staff in school or in the House (Year 7 girl).

Many girls also commented that they would talk things over with their parents. However many also said this would only happen as a last resort since many of the parents lived some distance away and would worry unnecessarily.

Nevertheless, the strongest recommendation was that the victim should be given advice on how to cope. This of course raises fundamental questions. Is there a general acceptance that verbal bullying is something human beings experience through life so that it is valuable to learn certain skills in order to survive? Or does fear of the issue coming out into the open mean that the girls want to learn to cope rather than complain about bullying? It matters little either way, since the girls wanted some form of procedure to operate in the school. Without bringing the topic into the curriculum, the girls would never have had the opportunity to air their views. Whatever the format or system of procedure decided upon by the staff in consultation with the girls is not particularly important, for the girls now had ownership of the procedure and system.

2.3 Further development

The girls recommended that advice and help should be provided in the House and in College. The advantage of seeing someone in College seemed to be the level of anonymity this allowed. Some suggested that the listener should be a sixth former. The sixth form girls are regarded with a certain amount of respect since they are in separate houses and there is only limited contact between them and the younger girls. Anonymity was felt to be crucial:

> *I think the best way is to have a box with a slit in the top into which you put a slip of paper with the bully's name on it. Your name is not on it. Then an appointed member of staff could take the name out. Then the bully would be watched carefully. This would give the victim more confidence than telling, as it is very hard to tell sometimes* (Year 8 girl).

Although such an approach clearly is flawed it highlights the pupils' concern over directly telling a member of staff. Nevertheless, there are ways around such problems. A few of the girls thought it would be helpful to have an adult in College to talk to. At this first stage the feeling was to have someone available who was not a member of the school's hierarchy, but someone who would simply listen, offer advice where necessary and not actively intervene.

> *At my old school there was a counsellor... And if you ever had a problem then you could arrange a time to share with the counsellor and she would discuss the problem and help you to solve it* (Year 8 girl).

The majority of girls commented that if they were being bullied they would first turn to their friends for help, usually in the same House as themselves and also some of the older girls.

> *The best way of helping someone who is being bullied is to get someone like a fifth former in every House to be someone who you can go to or talk to* (Year 9 girl).

> *The best way of helping someone who is being bullied is to tell someone older, who can sort it out* (Year 8 girl).

It was evident from the many comments that the girls do help each other, but of course the girl being bullied is often isolated and friendless; a channel of communications was needed to help such girls. To begin setting this up, Heads of Houses were called to a meeting along with girls in Year 11 to discuss the progress that had been made and the girls' revelations. After much discussion the girls decided that they would like to take a much more active role within the House to help girls who complained of being bullied. The girls commented that if they were to support others effectively in the

Supporting the victims of bullying
Outline of training session for Upper 5s

Time: approx 1 1/2 hours   Date:

1. Introduction
a) Briefing:

most common types of bullying at MGC; possible causes and likely personalities, feelings and reactions created;

b) Video — an example:

a victim reflects on his experiences; possible action by victim, teachers and parents.

2. Response: what is the U5 role?
a) General:

Watch for signs of bullying, taking responsibility, encouraging others to respond.

b) Specific:

how to deal with a request for help —

    find a suitable location (be sensitive)

    take note (look and listen)

    respond (ask, sympathise, encourage, care)

    act (discuss, suggest, review, inform (?)).

c) Particular considerations:

confidentiality — Who else to talk to about the situation, known your limitations. When and how to pass on information follow-up. How to offer continuing support while a situation is being sorted out.

3. Conclusion
Review — What is the role of the U5 team?
Where are the boundaries?

Support — What care is available to the team?
How could/should they use it?

Agree date for follow-up meeting to monitor progress.

House they needed some form of guidance and training. This was duly arranged.

After this meeting the School Chaplain was duly informed of the decision. She has a pastoral role within the school and agreed to run a training session for the girls. This course will become an annual event for all girls who hold positions of responsibility in the Middle School Houses.

2.4 Conclusion

Discussion on bullying at Malvern Girls College took place against the background of the introduction of the Children Act. One of the recommendations of the Act is that all boarding schools appoint an independent listener to help and advise pupils.

> It is important that provision is made for contact with an adult outside the school's structure including telephone Help Lines where appropriate for those situations where an element of confidentiality or independence is needed (3.11.1).

To combine the ideas of the girls with the requirements of the Act, a counsellor comes into school on a weekly basis. The girls have access to the counsellor without any reference to staff and can contact her by telephone.

It is hoped that by the start of the next academic year all these separate strands will have been drawn together and a coherent policy and procedures published for distribution to parents and girls. In many ways, the writing out of a formal document will appear unnecessary, but if it helps just one girl then it will have been worth the time. Without this imaginative curricular approach to combating bullying it is unlikely that the issue could have developed in the positive way that it took in this school. The curricular approach also meant that the efforts of the girls could be harnessed to combat bullying without the intervention of the staff.

3. Pensby High School for Boys, Wirral

Glyn Davies, Deputy Headteacher

The approach adopted at Pensby can be said to be curricular in its widest sense. Anything which happens in a school in terms of resources, staff development, management structures and decisions, organisation, assessment procedures, monitoring and so on, can be interpreted as having an effect upon curricular provision for the pupils. In this case the strategy adopted was a whole staff approach, and this inevitably had an impact upon the curriculum, the way in which it was delivered and its content.

Pensby High School for Boys is an 11 to 18 school with 680 pupils on roll. It is situated in the popular residential area of the Wirral; the catchment area is mainly private housing. Each year a percentage of higher ability pupils is creamed off to attend the local grammar school or to go into private education. Patterns of behaviour among the boys reflect the community's perception of them. Many of the boys are viewed as 'second class', since they did not 'pass' for other schools. This attitude is not apparent in the parents, however.

3.1 The beginnings

To tackle the problem of bullying the staff attended a training day (led by one of the editors of this book), which helped to develop broad strategies, identifying key areas of concern and, most importantly, involve all the staff. Detailed planning was then undertaken by a staff working party which produced the final document. To ensure that the document was accepted as official policy it was placed in the school development plan. This ensured that bullying would be monitored through on-going school assessment procedures.

It is perhaps a mark of the easy working atmosphere at Pensby that the school decided to tackle the problem of bullying in a questioning and realistic way. The matter was raised through the normal channels of the evaluation of school standards, not only in academic and behavioural terms, but also in a genuine caring for the individual happiness of each boy. Through the development of programmes in such areas as PSE, Life Skills, Drama and the use of pupil self-evaluation, awareness of the boys of their own worth and of their relationships with their peers had increased. This was in addition to excellent pastoral provision for the boys. However, it became clear that despite the good nature of most of the boys and the high standards of general discipline linked to it, there did exist for some boys a real or imaginary pressure from their peers. This was judged unacceptable and a planned programme was devised to combat the bullying in school. The implementation of that programme contributed directly to the delivery of the school aims for every pupil.

3.2 Implementation

Since Religious Education concerns the understanding of personal relationships and care for others, this was one of the foundation blocks of the anti-bullying programme and an integral part of the plan. With a variety of materials, the PSE Department has built up the means for the boys to express their ideas and thoughts about relationships and develop their interpersonal skills. The growth of drama within the school had further enhanced the scope of this department. The policy of beginning PSE in Year 7 and continuing the process throughout the school careers of the boys influenced the atmosphere in the school in a positive way. Relationships between pupils and between pupils and staff were improved. The traditional use of assembly time to heighten the sense of common purpose was reinforced by increased contributions by staff and pupils. Other areas of the curriculum may not have the words 'relationships', 'understanding', 'tolerance' and so on, written into their documents, but when opportunities arise, all staff are expected to use them to develop ideas on the fact that relationships are involved in all aspects of school life.

As well as this general approach the following procedure was adopted: all staff must watch for early signs of distress in pupils — deterioration of work, dubious illness, staying close to staff or supervisors at lunchtime. All incidents must be reported to form or year tutors and also any suspicions of bullying. Every time there is an incident, all staff must immediately make it clear that this level of behaviour is completely unacceptable. The form or year tutor must ensure that the bullied pupil records the events in writing and that the bully also does so. Thereafter, there must be a follow-up discussion with the boys. If the bullying is a recurrence then the notes must be sent to the bully's parents, via the year tutor. If a boy is continually under pressure from his peers, his parents must be informed. Where appropriate, the incident must be discussed with the year group or tutor group. The reaction of other boys is the most positive resource in the long-term attack on bullying.

To raise the awareness of the boys and to encourage them to become more active in the combating of bullying, the following steps were taken. During assemblies the following points were explained and positive reinforcement expected during tutor periods:

- ■ Why the issue is being highlighted.
- ■ What bullying really is and the insidious ways in which it works.
- ■ What the bullied person feels.

■ When someone is bullied others must react and inform the appropriate people.

■ The boys must not tolerate bullies.

■ Some boys accuse others of bullying after they have provoked the situation. This cannot be tolerated.

The 'tone' of a school is determined by the staff and the following points were underlined by the working party:

■ Staff should avoid using nicknames even when they are commonly used by the boys.

■ All boys have the right to personal dignity.

■ Even gentle banter between staff and boys must be carefully regulated. Boys might be quietly offended and unable to express their feelings in case they are punished for rudeness.

■ It is appreciated that care can be interpreted as being 'soft' but this is an essential part of the professional expertise expected of staff.

■ When staff have a supervisory duty covering a high risk area, they must ensure that they have a high profile.

■ The school ensures that all Year 7 boys start their secondary education with a short residential course on building relationships within the tutor group. This is supported by long-standing outdoor pursuit courses in the Lake District, the Duke of Edinburgh's Award activities and other residential courses. All these help to foster trust and mutual support. A school forum has recently been developed to add a further dimension to staff- pupil relationships. It will be used to draw out further ideas and develop those already listed.

3.3 Evaluation

This is still problematic, since there has been no audit of the extent of bullying within the school. Nevertheless, ongoing evaluation has taken place during tutor periods, pastoral meetings and in the school forum. The number of incidents that have come to light have also been monitored. By writing down the incidents as they occur, the staff can build a picture of the behaviour of the boys. This can then be reviewed at regular intervals. At the end of the school year the working party reconvened to review the progress with an appraisal of the original objectives.

Such an approach must of itself impact upon the curriculum. As Marland (1989) aptly comments:

> Guidance and support of the most individual kind depends on facts, understanding and skills. There are properly times across the curricu-

lum when facts and concepts are paramount and self-reflection less important — but one never completely abandons the other.

In the development of the anti-bullying programme at Pensby, the staff have attempted to put in place a set of procedures and a curriculum where the importance of the individual is paramount, without losing sight of the knowledge, skills and understanding needed for life in the 21st Century.

4. Editors' Commentary

Although the schools featured in this curriculum theme have produced some imaginative and ingenious ways of using curriculum content to help combat bullying, they have arrived at them more by chance than through careful planning. If we are to deliver the National Curriculum to pupils at the same time as making an anti-bullying curriculum accessible to all, without the threat of fear or humiliation, we need a carefully planned delivery of the curriculum.

To begin with, there needs to be a careful audit of present curricular provision. In the primary sector this is relatively simple, since curriculum delivery is usually controlled by one person — the class teacher. However, in the secondary sector this is rarely the case. The curriculum needs to be divided into two sections:

- The cognitive section, dealing with knowledge, understanding and the required academic skills, classified by the NCC as study skills, communication skills, IT skills, problem solving skills and numeracy skills.

- The affective section, dealing with attitudes and personal and social skills. These skills are fostered through the cross-curricular themes in the National Curriculum — Environmental Education, Guidance and Careers, Citizenship, Health Education and Education for Industrial Understanding. These themes make up diverse parts of the curriculum and although content free in themselves they appear in the core and foundation subjects in many guises.

However, neither the cognitive nor the affective curriculum have any meaning without the development of self. The curriculum which fails to place the development of the individual child at the centre of its delivery is working in a vacuum. As Tattum and Tattum (1992a) point out, the self can only be realised in a social context. In this extract from *Doctor Zhivago,* Yury explains to his ailing mother-in-law:

Well what are *you?* That's the crux of the matter. Let's try to find out. What is it about you that you have always known as yourself? What are you conscious of in yourself? Your kidneys? Your liver? Your blood vessels? No. However far back you go in your memory, it is always in some external, active manifestation of yourself that you come across your identity — in the work of your hands, in your family, in other people. And now look. You in others are yourself, your soul. This is what you are. This is what your consciousness has breathed and lived on and enjoyed throughout your life. — Your soul, your immortality, your life in others. (B.Pasternak)

This is what the individual pupil is — a social being. If we concentrate on the cognitive and lose sight of the affective, we are in danger of delivering a worthless curriculum. Of course, we have to provide the scientists, economists, technicians of the future, but we must never forget that these are people; our aim is to educate people. This letter makes the point admirably:

> Dear Teacher,
>
> I am a survivor of a concentration camp. My eyes saw what no man should witness:
>
> Gas chambers built by learned engineers. Children poisoned by educated physicians. Infants killed by trained nurses. Women and babies burnt and shot by high school and college graduates. So I am suspicious of education.
>
> My request is:
>
> Help your students become human. Your efforts must never produce learned monsters, skilled psychopaths, educated Eichmanns. Reading, writing, arithmetic are important only if they serve to make our children more human.
>
> —*Discovered on the noticeboard in a Headteacher's study in a Bradford secondary school.*

Schools, therefore, have systematically to make provision for the effective delivery of the affective curriculum and not neglect the moral and spiritual elements of each individual pupil's education.

To accomplish this, secondary schools must map not only the delivery of the cognitive curriculum but also the affective curriculum. The aims must be made abundantly clear: to promote and support the personal development of the individual, emotionally, socially, intellectually and spiritually. Individuals must be educated as active and responsible members of several communities — the family, the school, as well as local, national and global communities, so that all pupils learn to play an active role in society. As teachers we must support the processes of teaching and learning by developing personal and social skills, building self-esteem, valuing others and promoting positive attitudes. This can only be achieved by employing a variety of learning styles to enable pupils to practise these important personal and social skills within the classroom. These aims are consistent with the five cross-curricular themes outlined by the NCC and include the knowledge, skills and attitudes required to promote effective learning in a developmental way.

Separate departments, faculties or individual teachers need to take stock of these themes, and consider how they can be delivered by carefully choosing the cognitive content. For example, in Economic and Industrial Education, how are we to deliver controversial issues, including the role of governments and their economic policies, the impact of economic activity on the environment, issues relating to inequalities, poverty and the role of the EC? In Environmental Education we need to take into consideration a comparison of pupils' own environment with that of others. In Careers and Guidance we must explore ways in which individual goals can be set, how pupils manage their time and resources, and make them aware of opportunities that exist. In Citizenship, pupils need to consider the benefits, difficulties and conflicts inherent in living in a pluralist society. Pupils need to consider aspects of safety at home, on the roads, at school, at work and in their leisure time as part of a planned programme of Health Education. Not all appear all the time. However, if we map out where these elements appear through a pupil's school career, we can be sure that these areas are covered sufficiently thoroughly. Consider one concrete example:

The novel *Gowie Corby Plays Chicken* by Gene Kemp is useful to read with pupils at Key Stage Three. Let us assume that the pupils have just read chapters three and four, which contain accounts of some bullying. They could be asked to complete the following tasks in groups of four or five:

■ How do you feel about Gowie at the end of chapter four?
■ Why do you feel this way?
■ In what ways, if any, has Gowie changed?
■ In what ways, if any, have your views about Gowie changed?

The pupils must supply evidence from the text to support their views. They report their opinions back to the rest of the class. The pupils can then be asked to consider:

■ How can we deal with bullies or gangs or unpleasant incidents in school?

The opinions of the pupils can be distilled through consensus to develop a document, using a word processor or DTP package to present to the rest of the school. The whole class could develop an assembly to present to their year group or the whole school. Poetry could be brought in here, pupils justifying their selections for inclusion in an assembly. Posters could be designed for display in the assembly and around school.

By addressing the novel in this way we are covering large elements of the curriculum. Firstly, the English attainment targets are being delivered:

- Speaking and Listening — pupils are practising these skills in a variety of contexts, speaking to groups, speaking to a class, speaking to a large gathering of people in assembly. The pupils must also practise active listening if they are to come to a consensus.

- Writing — pupils can write in a variety of ways, producing imaginative work or reports about countering bullying generated by pupils themselves, not adults. Reports written using IT serve a far wider audience than the classroom teacher. Inevitably, pupils check their presentation carefully before their work goes into the public domain.

- Reading — the pupils read the novel, but also other aspects of the written word — newspaper articles, poetry, reference books or magazine articles on the subject.

Yet this is not all such a series of lessons can achieve. To work effectively in groups, pupils must co-operate and collaborate, covering aspects of Citizenship. They must work within a limited and pre-determined time scale, covering aspects of Guidance and Careers. They must develop and practise personal and social skills. They must solve problems and use IT to help them do so. The work need not stop here nor be limited to English lessons.

Further work can be incorporated into the delivery of Technology. If the pupils were to develop a questionnaire about the use of the playground, the information provided by it could be used in Maths, in the form of handling and presenting data or other practical applications. From the information gathered, pupils will have identified a need within the school — improving the environment in which they play. Design proposals to change specific areas of the playground can be generated and artefacts made and evaluated. This covers areas of Environmental Education and Health Education, as well as reinforcing the personal and social skills mentioned earlier.

This is not an exhaustive list of what can be done in school, nor is it intended to be. It merely suggests what can be achieved, with imagination and careful planning. Importantly, it gives pupils some choice over their own education, helps to develop self-esteem and sense of personal worth — their ideas are being asked for and implemented. This sense of personal worth can be reinforced further by incorporating Records of Achievement into the programme. The individual achievements of pupils can be formalised, so strengthening the development of self.

It is important to note that it is not simply *what* is delivered in this view of the curriculum, but *how* it is delivered that is important and needs to be planned. Also important is a clear statement of realistic aims for the process. If the aims and objectives are set out clearly in terms of both the cognitive and the affective curriculum, then pupils' work can be effectively evaluated.

If certain areas of requisite knowledge have been left untouched by the delivery of such a module, these should be covered as pupils progress through the school, or in a subsequent module.

The schools mentioned above have gone a long way to meeting the criteria formalised here. Other schools may find it useful to begin their review of curricular delivery by looking at the organisation of pupils within the school and considering what implicit messages are received by pupils because of it. Whatever the starting point, there needs to be this initial audit, followed by planned delivery of the curriculum in both its cognitive and affective elements. The separate core and foundation subjects must be looked at not only in terms of their content but in how that content is delivered. Finally, the cross-curricular themes and skills need to be mapped to ensure that the development of the concept of self remains at the heart of the curriculum. In this way we can begin to educate our children so that they become 'more human'.

Theme Three

Transition

Introduction

The most threatening times in a pupil's school career are associated with transition. Transition does not necessarily mean from junior to secondary phase; it can mean from infant to primary or from pre-school to schooling. All are important changes in a child's development and socialisation. Rumours abound about 'initiation ceremonies':

> *'You will be thrown over the wall.'*
> *'You will have your dinner poisoned.'*
> *'You will have your head pushed down the toilet.'*
> *'You will be covered in shaving foam.'*

Although there is little danger of such things actually happening, the fear they induce is all too real. If pupils are frightened on arrival at school or in a lesson, there is little point in trying to deliver a curriculum to them. Fear will be dominant and education will have little meaning. Research surveys into pupil transfer, summarised by the table below, reveal that bullying figures prominently in every survey.

If the transition is not a smooth process, it can often be the beginnings of a deviant career, as both work and behaviour suffer. This can follow the pupil until s/he leaves school. The schools whose approaches are outlined below

Anxieties about Transfer:what researchers have found to worry pupils most				
Galton & Willcocks (1986)	Hamblin (1978)	Youngman & Lunzer (1977)	Davies (1986)	Measor & Woods (1984)
Bullying Separation from friends Size of School	Homework Exams New Teachers Bullying Size of School	Things stolen Losing things School Work Exams Bullying	Bullying Specific subjects Getting lost Homework	Size of School New work demands Losing friends Bullying New forms of discipline and authority

© Delwyn & Eva Tattum 1992

could equally illustrate other approaches. For example, the work at Lakeside relates to the curriculum approach outlined earlier. The Lakeside report also shows how primary schools find it easier than secondary schools to deliver the cross-curricular themes. Of special interest is that four different models are outlined. Of the two secondary schools, one, South Craven, concentrates on a cluster approach. The other, Minsthorpe, concentrates on the development of a pyramid approach. Lakeside, a primary school, highlights the difficulties of transition that can arise even within one institution. Finally, Millfield School highlights the particular problems faced by boarders and the variety of ways in which bullying can be successfully tackled in similar institutions.

All these schools offer accounts of successful attempts to counter bullying across the age range 4-18. Similar themes occur in each. One is the pupils' perception of what constitutes bullying behaviour: all viewed it as any behaviour by one or more pupils which caused unhappiness in others. The measures adopted by the schools also show similar approaches, particularly of giving pupils confidence to tell someone about their problems. All the schools were conscious of their pupils' fear of bullying and acted to overcome them, particularly fears associated with transition.

1. Lakeside Primary School, Cardiff

Richard Coleman, Deputy Headteacher

The school was built in 1961 as separate Infant and Junior schools with nine infant and 12 junior classes. At one time, well over 600 pupils were accommodated. The two schools were amalgamated in 1981 into one primary school with just over 400 pupils taught in six infant and eight junior classes. The building, built mainly of brick with lots of glass, is large for a primary school. The Infant Department is all on ground level and separated from the Junior Department by a large kitchen. The Junior Department is a large three-storey building and the top junior classes are on the top floor.

Catchment is from an area of mostly owner-occupied detached and semi-detached houses built in the early 1960s. A large proportion of the parents have a business or professional background. There are about 60 pupils for whom English as a second language, mostly from outside the catchment area. The majority of these pupils originate from the Indian sub-continent although there is a wide variety of ethnicities and cultures. It is not unusual for pupils to be admitted to the school on arrival in Britain, having little or no knowledge of English.

The school has three playgrounds (two junior and one infant) and in dry weather the children can play on the extensive grassed areas surrounding the buildings. The common inner city problem of congested playgrounds does not apply at Lakeside. The pupils have plenty of room to run and escape from any pupils they do not wish to be near. However, this gives rise to another problem — there are so many different play areas that the staff have difficulty keeping an eye on everybody at all times. It is easy for pupils who wish to hide, to do so.

1.1 The beginnings

The initiative by Lakeside primary was inspired by two sources. Firstly, in discussion with Year 6 pupils, staff learned that bullying was a major concern about their forthcoming transfer to secondary school The second stimulus came from the Headteacher who was helping to produce a series of videos about bullying.

Pupils in the school face three major transitions: from home to school, from infant to junior department and from junior to secondary school. Starting school is a crucial step in a child's personal and social development and for this reason alone it should be thoroughly planned and prepared for. Some children learn about school from older siblings but many learn from some form of pre-schooling, the value of which lies not so much in academic gains but in helping young children adjust to being with other children who may be more competitive, demanding or aggressive. Nursery schools are not immune from bullying. Lakeside has a fully integrated programme for involving parents of new pupils, recognising, as it does, the value of first contacts in securing good home-school foundations.

This initiative was started in the summer term, concerned primarily with school to school transfer. Because of the physical structure of the school, the Infant Department is divided from the Junior Department by the kitchens. Pupils are forbidden to use the route through the kitchen for health and safety reasons. This means that despite the efforts of the staff to integrate the two departments, many of the Year 2 pupils talk about moving up to the 'big school' with anxiety. They told their teacher that they were worried about being 'jumped on' in the toilets, about having their games spoiled by older pupils and that their dinners might be taken from them in the dining room. These were expressions of real concern, which the school felt it had to tackle.

Transfer within the school was something which the staff felt they could control, as teachers work closely for the good of all the pupils. Information is shared both formally and informally. Staff are aware, however, that for their Year 6 pupils the move to secondary school was something over which the school had less control. Over the years the school has worked closely with the secondary school to devise a programme of preparatory visits to ease the settling-in process. The pupils face transfer with a mixture of excitement and apprehension. They are hesitant about leaving the familiar small school for the much larger comprehensive, though they look forward to the challenge of new subjects, specialist facilities and going to the 'big school', with all that it means in the signifying of maturity.

From contact with the Head of Lower School, staff are aware that most of their former pupils settle into their new school without much fuss; but this does not mean that they do not have their worries. Those who are anxious can be unhappy and unsuccessful, for these early experiences can adversely affect their subsequent time in school. The seeds of underachievement and disaffection can be sown during this critical transfer period. This is why the school has an induction programme, to alleviate commonly expressed concerns.

1.2 Further developments

The Deputy Headteacher invited the teachers of classes in Years 2, 5 and 6 — six teachers in all — to a meeting to discuss the proposed project. They discussed how the project should develop and which cross-curricular elements each class should concentrate on, to avoid duplication and also allow for a wide range of ideas to be trialled. Everyone agreed that bullying was part of the unpleasant side of school life which should be tackled and that a school-wide project would stimulate pupils to talk and staff to think about the problem. It was also agreed that the school's curriculum was a positive way of influencing pupils' views about bullying and of examining their preconceptions of what kinds of children become bullies and who become victims of bullies.

One interesting outcome was the various ways in which the staff saw most areas of the curriculum becoming involved. The subjects involved were:

English (poetry, story writing and drama)
Maths
Design and Technology
Art
RE

One colleague pointed out that the project fitted well with the school's planning of its Personal and Social Education Programme.

In summary, the contribution of each class was to be:

Year 2   Class 1   Story writing and telling
           Class 2   Drama and Art work

Year 5   Class 1   A school survey into bullying
           Class 2   Preparing a morning
                        assembly for the whole school

Year 6   Class 1   Poetry and story writing
           Class 2   Ideas about stereotypes of
                        bullies and victims
                        A board game based on
                        bullying

1.3 Implementation

Year Six

The two Year 6 teachers decided to invite three former pupils, now at the local comprehensive school, to talk to their classes about their experiences of transfer. Two girls and a boy from Year 8 agreed and, with their school's permission, spent part of a morning with some Year 6 pupils. The staff chose Year 8 rather than Year 7 pupils for several reasons. They thought that Year 7 pupils would be the ones most likely to be spreading rumours about bullying and even organising the initiation rituals on the basis that they wished to perpetuate the myth that 'It happened to us!'. Moreover, Year 8 pupils were more distant in age from the primary pupils and would appear more responsible and mature so their advice would be more readily accepted.

The three youngsters turned out to be very reassuring and positive. They described their own experiences and answered questions from the younger children.

Ann told the classes, 'Being called names and teasing worried me at the time. I was also worried about any stuff being taken, like my calculator. So make sure you write your name on all your equipment and look after all your property.'

David's advice was, 'If you have any problems tell a teacher. That's the main message — If anything happens tell your form teacher or any other teacher and they will usually sort it out for you.'

They talked about school being enjoyable if you go with a positive attitude. Their visit stimulated a lot of discussion and work around the theme of bullying. Class 1, for instance, had an intense discussion about bullies. Their teachers had no doubt that bullying is a problem that affects the quality of life of many pupils in schools. Her class chose to write a short story or a poem from personal experience (where possible). Here is one which seems to come from the heart:

Bullies

A bully is like a headache banging on your brain,
You cringe with fear as he thumps harder,
'Leave me alone' you shout,
A bully is a ghost haunting you for life.

Class 2's teacher divided his class into five groups, each to work on different aspects of the project.

Group 1   Facts and Fiction about bullying

This group decided to draw up a list of common anxieties about what bullying is under the headings *Fact* and *Fiction*. Here are some of their ideas:

Fact	Fiction
Stealing your money	Locking you in the toilet
Name-calling	Pushing you into the staffroom
Giving wrong directions	Putting heroin in your burgers

Group 2   The characteristics of a bully

Members of this group drew a caricature of a bully. They also made fact and fiction lists about what a bully looks like.

In the end the group's message was that a bully looks the same as anyone else.

Group 3 Advice

This group of girls spent a long time drawing up the following useful advice for pupils who find that they are being bullied;

1. Ignore them.
2. Say no if they tell you to do something.
3. Stay with friends.
4. Fight back.
5. Make them feel ashamed.
6. Get other advice eg. from ChildLine or Helpline.
7. Stay away from the places where the bullies hang out.
8. Parents and teachers can work together.

Their advice was practical and useful, although advising children to fight back poses a dilemma for teachers.

Group 4 Vocabulary

This group decided to do some vocabulary work using the letters in the word BULLY. The exercise generated a lot of language work and negotiation about which group of words best described a bully.

B — *Brutal*
U — *Unfriendly*
L — *Loathsome*
L — *Lout*
Y — *Yob*

Group 5 Board Game

The final group worked on a board game centred around bullying. This was a complicated practical task, requiring them to divide the board into squares, draw and print instructions and make markers and bully cards. The exercise also challenged them intellectually, to devise items and consequences for every square. Examples of their ideas are:

1. Caught by a bully — pick up a bully card.
2. Caught by a bully gang — lose a turn.
3. Tell your mother about the bully — move on 3 places.

Year Five

In Year 5, Class 1 elected to prepare a morning assembly for the whole school on the theme of bullying. They put in a deal of work writing their own materials and researching suitable stories and poems. Here is an extract from their script, opening the assembly.

Child 1: *We are starting our assembly this morning by thinking about things which frighten us.*

Child 2: *We wrote poems with the title 'I Am Afraid'. Here are two of them.*

> *Poem 1*   *I am afraid*
> *I am afraid of ghosts spookily flying in a dark, old house,*
> *Or a gloomily deserted street where a bully might be around every corner.*
> *I am afraid of a nuclear power station bubbling in the night,*
> *And a man with a sharp axe swinging it wildly about.*

> *Poem 2*   *I am afraid*
> *I am afraid of the dog with lethal teeth, roaming recklessly along the street,*
> *And deadly insects crawling over me at night.*
> *I am afraid of the drunken tramp with his razor blade in a gloomy street on a dark night,*
> *And someone waiting for me outside school ready to attack me.*

Child 3: *I expect you noticed that the children were afraid of people as well as frightening places and situations. The theme of our assembly this morning is bullying. That's when somebody frightens or threatens someone else who is not as strong as they are.*

Child 4: *Perhaps one of these short scenes will remind you of something that you've seen or experienced not a million miles from this school hall.*

The assembly continued with three short sketches written by the children. They dealt with extortion — taking someone's sweets; with physical bullying — spoiling a game of football; with verbal bullying — calling someone 'Swot, swot, swot'.

The assembly closed as follows:

Child 5: *We'll close our assembly this morning with a prayer.*
Dear God, please give us the courage to stand up to bullies. Make us more aware of the feelings of others, Share with us your strength this day. Amen.

The message of the assembly was reinforced by a visit from a photographer and reporter from a local newspaper. An article, plus large photo appeared in the press later that week.

While Class 1 arranged the assembly, Class 2 decided to carry out a survey of bullying throughout the school of 250 pupils, via a questionnaire. After seeing Year 6 pupils' drawings of bullies they decided not to use the word 'bully' anywhere in the questionnaire. There were too many stereotyped

The Questionaire About Mean and Nasty Children

All the questions have been compiled by the children of Class 5C

Please answer all of the questions truthfully.
Draw a circle around the appropriate words where we give you a choice.
DO NOT WRITE YOUR NAME - we do not need it.
Please write your age and circle boy or girl for <u>each question</u> - this sheet will be cut up.

Boy Girl
Age ...
1. Have you ever been called names which upset you a lot ? YES NO
If yes, what names ?...

Boy Girl

Age ...
2.Have you ever been hurt by someone for no reason?   YES NO
If yes, were they :
A BOY   A GIRL
IN SCHOOL   OUTSIDE SCHOOL
YOUNGER THAN YOU   SAME AGE   OLDER THAN YOU

Boy Girl

Age ...
3.Have you ever been deliberately ignored by other children for a long time ?

YES   NO

Boy Girl

Age ...
4. Have you ever been threatened a lot by other children ? YES   NO
If yes, were they
A BOY   A GIRL
IN SCHOOL   OUTSIDE SCHOOL
YOUNGER THAN YOU   SAME AGE   OLDER THAN YOU

Boy Girl

Age ...
5. Where do the mean and nasty children hang around in school ?
....
or DON'T KNOW

Boy Girl

Age ...
6. Where do the mean and nasty children hang around outside school ?
....
or DON'T KNOW

Boy Girl

Age ...
7. When do the mean and nasty children cause trouble in school ?
(You can circle more than one answer if you want to)
BEFORE 9a.m.BELL   MORNING PLAY   LUNCHTIME
AFTERNOON PLAY   AFTER 3.45pm BELL   WET PLAYS
WHEN YOUR TEACHER IS OUT OF THE CLASSROOM

Boy Girl

Age ...
8. When do the mean and nasty children cause trouble outside school ?
(You can circle more than one answer if you want to)
WALKING TO SCHOOL   TO AND FROM SCHOOL AT LUNCHTIME
WALKING HOME FROM SCHOOL   WEEKENDS   HOLIDAYS

skinhead boys in scruffy jackets, for their liking. 'Most bullies don't look like that — they're more ordinary,' said one girl, 'and you get girl bullies too'.

To prevent stereotyped images being given to the children before they filled in the questionnaire, a new descriptive term was needed. After much discussion, the questionnaire was entitled 'A Questionnaire About Mean and Nasty Children'. Important decisions had to be made about the questions to be asked.

What information was required about the child filling in the questionnaire?

Was it important that the child remained anonymous?

How would the information gained be analysed and presented?

The pupils decided that names would not be asked for and that a statement be written into the questionnaire that names were not needed, lest pupils wrote their names on out of sheer habit. Two facts about the individual were, however, needed: their age and sex. All the information could have been put into a database but that would have taken a few pupils a long time. The class wanted to analyse the information quickly and all complete their work simultaneously.

The solution was to divide the A4 questionnaire into nine sections. Once completed and returned, they could be quickly guillotined into separate questions. Groups of three or four pupils were allocated to each question, to analyse the information on their separate slips of paper. Of course, once guillotined and distributed amongst the group, the sheets could not be put back together again, so the essential information of age and sex had to be incorporated into each question. This was achieved by putting 'B or G' next to each question, plus a box for the individual's age. The questions were discussed during one busy afternoon, involving everyone. The final wording was eventually decided upon by the pupils themselves. Anything controversial was decided by voting.

Was the questionnaire to be written by a child and photocopied? No! The class decided as one. It had to be typed and duplicated by the School Secretary just like a letter to their parents, so that it looked authentic and official. Questionnaires were distributed, completed and collected on the same day. Sheets were guillotined as soon as they had been checked for correct completion of details of age and sex. The analysis started in earnest. Only one group needed very much teacher's help — the question: 'Have you ever been called names which upset you and if so what names?' Some pupils had been considerate about the possible embarrassment of the researchers when writing names they had been called and had written the first letter only of the more obvious four-letter words. Others were more frank and provided the researchers with a wealth of obscenities, often impeccably spelt! What should be done? A fine balance had to be kept between maintaining a degree of reality and at the same time shielding ten year olds from a stream of offensive words.

The solution decided was both simple and effective. Any word which in its dictionary sense was not a swear word would remain uncensored by the teacher's black marker pen eg. 'bitch', 'cow', 'bloody'. Words which had no meaning other than as obscenity were obliterated after recording their occurrence. Two days later, the 250 questionnaires were a pile of paper strips in the recycling box and a fine collection of histograms and pie charts were ready for display.

Year Two

In Year 2, Class 1 started the week with an 'on the mat' chat about going up to the Juniors and all the things the children thought might or would happen. The talk moved from what they looked forward to, to what worried them. That was when several children brought up the possibility of being bullied, without any prompting from their teacher. A great deal of discussion then centred around places where children might be a little frightened. The class then wrote their own ideas of what bullying could be.

In Class 2, the teacher concentrated on Art and Drama. The children produced a colourful collage using a range of words to do with bullying.

The class also wrote a short play about telling their parents if they were bullied and performed it for the whole Infant Department.

1.4 Evaluation

The value of the project was in both its cross-curricular approach and the fact that it affected every child in the school. For some it generated a great deal of work; for others it meant involvement in a large scale and detailed survey of their opinions and experiences. Other pupils watched scenes they themselves had perhaps witnessed portrayed in the assembly.

For a week, the one topic of conversation was common in playground and staffroom. It was this joint raising of awareness of the problem for both pupils and staff that was one of the project's strengths and from which further work could be developed. Everyone knew that bullying happened, but many of the adults were surprised by the frequency of the problem, that girls were so often involved and that it extended much further than physical bullying. Staff, pupils, governors and parents saw the results of the project and were compelled to think about some of the many issues raised.

As for the bullies? Yes, they are in this school, just as in every school in the country, but they are now being talked about a lot more than they like.

2. South Craven High School, West Yorkshire

Stephen Wilkinson,Deputy Headteacher
Jacky Dickenson, Head of Year
Karen Watson, Head of Year

Transition problems are also tackled in an imaginative and positive way by South Craven High School in West Yorkshire, taking not merely a whole-school but a whole-cluster approach.

South Craven School is a large 11-18 comprehensive, with 1,700 pupils on roll. Half its intake comes from the Metropolitan District of Bradford, the other half from more rural North Yorkshire. There are ten 'official' feeder schools, ranging from small village primary schools near the Pennine Way, to larger schools in the urban districts.

The cluster of primary schools is well served by a committee comprising their Headteachers plus a Deputy Headteacher and the Head of Lower School of South Craven School. One of the main functions of this committee is to provide smooth transition between Key Stages two and three. This committee takes a high profile, not only in terms of National Curriculum delivery, but also in terms of pupil welfare. It was therefore no surprise when the suggestion of a joint approach to a 'Cluster Policy' on bullying was well received. Since the raising of the problem, bullying has become an important issue for:

> Heads of Year
> Year 7 and 8 Council
> Primary Cluster Meetings
> Transition from feeder to secondary schools
> Equal Opportunities forum
> Behaviour Policy
> Personal and Social Development
> INSET Programmes

2.1 The beginnings

As part of the induction process, the Head of Year 7 visited all the feeder schools and took part in lessons which gave an opportunity for informal communication with Year 6 pupils and a chance to find out what, if anything, concerned them about their move to secondary school. Their main concern was that they would be bullied by older pupils. Some were convinced that organised gangs tracked down new Year 7 pupils with the intention of performing unspecified but dreadful initiation rites. The Head of Year

QUESTIONNAIRE

I am a boy ☐   I am a girl ☐

Age ☐   Year ☐

During this week another pupil:

	No	Once	More than once
1. Helped me with my homework			
2. Called me names			
3. Said something nice to me			
4. Teased me about my family			
5. Tried to kick me			
6. Was very nice to me			
7. Teased me because I am different			
8. Gave me a present			
9. Threatened to hurt me			
10. Gave me some money			
11. Demanded money from me			
12. Tried to frighten me			
13. Asked me a stupid question			
14. Lent me something			
15. Told me off			
16. Teased me			
17. Talked about clothes with me			
18. Told me a joke			
19. Told me a lie			
20. Ganged up on me			

	No	Once	More than once
21. Tried to make me hurt other people			
22. Smiled at me			
23. Tried to get me into trouble			
24. Helped me carry something			
25. Tried to hurt me			
26. Helped me with my class work			
27. Made me do something I didn't want to			
28. Talked about T.V. with me			
29. Took something off me			
30. Shared something with me			
31. Was rude about the colour of my skin			
32. Shouted at me			
33. Played a game with me			
34. Tried to trip me up			
35. Talked about interests with me			
36. Laughed at me			
37. Threatened to tell on me			
38. Tried to break something of mine			
39. Told a lie about me			
40. Tried to hit me			

reassured them that in the twenty years she had taught in the school, nothing like that had ever happened.

However, no-one had any idea of how much bullying went on in the school, or in what ways it manifested itself. An action plan was developed (see Action Plan, page 99).

This began with a questionnaire distributed to Years 5 and 6 of the cluster primary schools and Years 7, 8 & 9 of the secondary school (see page 97).

All pupils filled in the questionnaire without prior discussion so with no preconceived ideas of what their teachers thought bullying was. Since the survey size was so large (over 1000 pupils) only a sample of the results was collated. Nevertheless, the findings proved illuminating. The highest incidence of bullying was among Year 6 pupils, diminishing with age and Year 7 pupils feel more vulnerable than older pupils. These figures agree with other research findings in this country and abroad. Stephenson and Smith (1988) found that bullying was a major problem associated with pupils in their final year at primary school so did Roland (1988) in Norway.

There were also some interesting suggestions from all year groups about how to avoid being bullied:

Year 7-9: Do not make enemies ...avoid bullies ...ignore them ...walk away ...stay friendly ...tell someone

Years 5 and 6: Share with people ...be kind ...don't call others names ...stay with friends ...don't tease people ...go where there are a lot of teachers about.

2.2 Further developments

The personal and social development working party was looking at all aspects of PSE throughout the school. The aim was to include aspects of bullying in the cognitive and affective curricula, aiming for a progressive awareness of bullying through years 7 to 11. Pupils have timetabled PSE as well as programmes during tutorial time. The pastoral programme in Years 7, 8 and 9 allows time for form tutors to consider bullying as a topic. Work done during this time, along with the results of the survey, raised the awareness of both pupils and staff concerning the extent of bullying and its nature. This was reinforced by assemblies and a poster competition promoted by the Year 7 and 8 councils. Some examples of these posters are set out below (pages 100, 101).

The posters were displayed as an integral part of the school's 'Good Behaviour Week', during which the school launched its behaviour policy. Pupils were invited to prioritise and add to the list of 'Classroom Expectations' (see page 102).

BULLYING: PLAN OF ACTION

1. Issue a questionnaire to the whole school (Kidscape questionnaire) to collect data on the scale of the problem.

2. Write a school policy on bullying, to be issued to teachers, parents, NTA, lunch time supervisors, governors, feeder schools.

3. Methods of implementing the policy:

   a. Playgrounds need looking at. Not enough hard areas for students to play, not enough benches for children to sit.

   b. Staff training needed.

   c. Bullying counsellor in school available for students, possibly several times a week.

   d. Photographs of all staff, including NTAs, lunch-time supervisors, caretaking staff, with name and position of member of staff, posted in school entrance.

   e. Supervisory assistants must be involved and have a training session, possibly one lunch-time when *staff* would have to cover duties.

   f. Classroom rules written by students displayed in every room.

   g. Poster campaign around school — **We don't tolerate bullying. It's OK to tell.**

   h. Involve student council.

   i. Involve matron.

   j. Assertiveness training for victims.

   k. Give bullying a *high* profile.

CLASSROOM EXPECTATIONS OF STUDENTS

Classrooms (including laboratories, workshops and gyms) are places of work. Just as in any factory or office, rules and expectations need to be clearly understood to allow everyone to work successfully, safely and enjoyably.

1. **At the start of lessons, students should:**

- Enter rooms sensibly and go straight to your place.
- Take off and put away any outdoor wear.
- Take out books, pens and equipment.
- Remain silent during registration (except when your name is called!).

2. **During lessons, students should adhere to the following principles:**

- Remain silent and concentrate when teacher talks to the whole class.
- If the class is asked a question, put up your hand to answer: do not call out (unless are asked for quick ideas).
- Be sure to have pen, pencil, ruler, rough book and any books or folders needed.
- Work sensibly with your classmates: do not distract or annoy them.
- If you arrive late for no good reason, expect to stay in at break or lunchtime to make up the work missed.
- Homework must be recorded.
- Eating, drinking and chewing are not allowed: items found will be confiscated.
- Walkmans, radios, magazines or other distractions are not allowed: they will be confiscated.
- You must not leave a lesson without permission from a teacher.
- If you are working outside a classroom show consideration for others by working quietly.

Since the behaviour policy is predicated on courtesy, consideration for others and the belief that everyone in the school community has an important role, its condemnation of bullying is both implicit and explicit. Bullying is discouraged by the promotion of a school ethos where the reporting of bullying is not seen as telling tales. Pupils are encouraged to report incidents in the knowledge that they will be taken seriously and dealt with.

The school has already taken action in response to suggestions made by the school council. In discussion, pupils made it clear that they wanted a quiet area available at break and lunchtimes. Some pupils disliked the noise and activity of the playground. A reading and homework room has been provided, overseen by the council helped by the staff.

2.3 Future Developments

Further training days are planned to maintain momentum. The aim is to produce a school 'Bullying Policy' for distribution to the feeder primary schools, parents and governors.

The school has already presented its policies on Equal Opportunities and Special Needs which will be linked to the bullying policy. Assertiveness training courses are also planned for pupils known to be victims of bullying. The six one-hour sessions will start with a session on self-worth, in which pupils share and praise one another's achievements. Pupils will video re-enactments of such situations, then discus how these might be improved. The improved scenarios will be acted out and filmed, then improved further. The process will be evaluated by the school's Educational Psychologist.

The staff see the way forward in continuing awareness-raising as Key Stage 3 pupils move through the school. This can be achieved by developing pupil self-help groups and extending the anti-bullying programme to all the feeder primary schools.

3. Minsthorpe High School and Community College, West Yorkshire
Janet Blackburn, Deputy Headteacher

A different way of including the feeder schools in an anti-bullying programme is demonstrated at Minsthorpe High School. The school lies half a mile north of South Elmsall near the boundary of Wakefield Metropolitan District. The school serves a distinct catchment of the three townships of South Elmsall, South Kirby and Upton, all originally mining villages. Mining has declined over the last decade and the area is diversifying its industrial base. However, it maintains its 'tough' image, often using physical violence to chastise children and settle disputes. The school has worked hard at insisting that this approach is not acceptable.

The school was opened in 1968 as the first purpose-built 13-18 school in the country and local schools were re-organised into a three tier pyramid system. Additional facilities were added with funds from the Carnegie Trust, to provide a community dimension. There were once over 1400 pupils on roll, with over 400 in a Year Group. In 1992 there were 842 pupils on roll, with 140 in Years 12 & 13. The school is organised on a year group basis, each with a Head of Year and a team of tutors responsible for the general welfare of mixed-ability tutor groups. The tutors remain with their group from 13 to 16 so can give advice and help based upon considerable knowledge of individual pupils.

The community development work carried out by a small team consisting of the Head of Youth and Community, the Youth Tutor and the Community Tutor is a huge strength of the school. This team acts as a catalyst for the ideas, energies and compassion of many others in the community, mostly voluntary workers. Their aim is not simply to organise things for people but to empower them to recognise their own needs and find ways to provide them.

3.1 The beginnings

Bullying: A Positive Response was the starting point for the work at Minsthorpe. A great deal of pastoral work already went on in the school, some related to bullying, but not as a concerted effort on a wide front. The booklet was the stimulus for recognising that bullying was a whole-school issue and this had implications far beyond the school.

One important thrust in the school had been the strengthening of the pyramid, with improved links between Minsthorpe, the five feeder middle schools and the seven first schools. The suggestion that bullying should be one of the workshops at the Pyramid INSET day was readily accepted. A training day was organised, in which one of the editors was a keynote speaker.

A working party was set up specifically to produce a short-term policy document on bullying with a representative membership in terms of experience and responsibilities.

Progress has been largely due to the efforts of this initial working party, whose commitment was evident from the research time they devoted and their levels of involvement. The meetings became a source of inspiration. The group quickly identified that:

- As a 13-18 school, it needed the active support and help of the other schools in the Pyramid
- As a community school, it was fitting that bullying was tackled outside the school
- Producing a short-term policy would be far more demanding than was first realised.

Only after a great deal of preparatory work did the group feel confident to develop their ideas elsewhere in the school. The first few meetings were spent sharing ideas on a subject on which no-one felt expert, yet all felt strongly. The group was nevertheless pleased to find confirmation of their definitions and views about bullying and used some definitions to help launch the short-term policy below.

In their early discussions, staff realised that their ideas were based on mere assumptions and not facts. There was little reliable evidence for answers to such questions as: Where did bullying occur? When did it happen? Who was bullied? Who were the bullies? What were the pupils'

SHORT-TERM POLICY ON BULLYING

Underlying assumptions and aims:

1. All staff (teaching and non-teaching) share an understanding of what is defined as 'bullying'.

2. All staff respond with consistency.

3. Immediate action must be taken to intervene whenever bullying occurs.

4. Staff and students recognise the benefits of taking a stand against bullying.

5. Governors, parents and other members of the local community are aware of Minsthorpe's policy on bullying.

views? Staff ran a whole-school survey simultaneously with their other tasks, in order to provide such evidence.

Although the working party had been given the brief to produce a policy document, it was never intended that it did so in isolation. Concerned not to be seen as a secretive little group of experts with all the answers, the working party tried hard to canvass opinion from elsewhere, both formally and informally. They used staff room notice board, staff bulletins, staff briefings, other meetings to make staff aware of what was happening and also asked pupils for their opinions.

Staff were generally supportive, but some were critical initially, arguing that bullying happens and always will, so that trying to tackle it is a waste of time; or claiming that the working party was nothing more than a 'talking shop' producing little action whilst the problem continued. The working party was constantly wary of moving too quickly, lest the initiative be perceived as a passing fashion, soon forgotten, but had to respond to the staff's views reasonably promptly. A balance was reached and the policy launched after a term and a half's work.

3.2 Further developments

To broaden their horizons, the working party had used resources outside school — attending LEA INSET courses, National Conferences (eg. the 'Safer Schools, Safer Cities' project in Wolverhampton) and disseminating information from books such as *Bullying in Schools* by (Tattum and Lane 1988). A great deal of deliberation took place over the use of the word 'intervention'. All too often bullying incidents are ignored as trivial, yet the working party made the fundamental assumption that if all 'minor' incidents were tackled then those agreed to be 'major' would occur less frequently and the school would be creating a more caring, safe environment. So the need for constant intervention was stressed: it would have an effect on the bullies, the victims and — just as importantly — the spectators.

When the working party had drawn up its third draft document, it decided, with encouragement from the Educational Psychologist, to launch it. The success of the document depended on its enabling staff to deal with situations themselves; in other words, on giving them confidence to intervene.

A survey had been drawn up by two members of the working party to provide staff with concrete evidence about the nature of bullying in their school, (see the end of this section). It was decided to involve all pupils from Years 9-13 in the survey and to give no advance warning. The survey was conducted in tutor groups, so each Head of Year had the opportunity to go through the questionnaire with the tutor team, who would then have the responsibility for explaining to the pupils the importance of the survey and the reasons for completing it. Results were collated by a member of the maths

Administrative stages in dealing with bullying

1. Staff should intervene,whatever the intensity of the bullying.

2. The priority is to give protection and support to the victim.

3. Staff must make it clear to bullies that their behaviour is totally unacceptable.

4. Staff should make it clear to onlookers that bullying will not be tolerated in the school.

5. All incidents, however trivial, should be reported to Tutors. Tutors will be responsible for ensuring that Heads of Year know every aspect involving students' behaviour.

6. If a serious bullying incident occurs in a classroom, Heads of Department, or the Senior Staff Support System via the General Office, should be called for additional assistance when needed.

7. When a serious incident occurs outside the classroom:

   - intervention is vital and disapproval must be expressed
   - the victim must receive support and protection
   - names or recognisable features of those involved must be obtained
   - the victim should be taken away from the scene
   - help should be obtained from HoY/DHoY or Senior Staff Support.

8. Parents of both bullies and victims should be made aware of any serious incident and advised how their actions might help. Tutors, in consultation with HOY or DHoY, should be involved in repeated incidents.

9. Through the HoY, the Police Juvenile Liaison Officer could where appropriate be called on for advice and support.

10. Students must be informed about:

   - places they can go during non-teaching time, where they can feel safe
   - who they can contact for support at any time during the day.

department who, after painstakingly analysing the data and presenting it in the form of pie charts and histograms, impressed on the working party the need to find a questionnaire which was easier to collate!

Some of the insights provided were illuminating, especially in Years 9, 10 and 11 where the majority of the bullying was reported — and particularly about bullying tactics employed by staff! The fact that 82.5% of pupils in Year 9, 67.5% of Year 10 and 70% of Year 11 were willing to talk and write about bullying at first seemed reassuring, but further responses generated concern. When asked whom they would talk to, the vast majority indicated a friend. Only 39% of pupils in Year 9 admitted they were prepared to talk to a teacher. In Year 10 it dropped to 33% and in Year 11 to only 20%. At the time, pupils may have had little confidence in the staff's desire or ability to intervene effectively. Among pupils who admitted to telling no-one in school, most said it only made matters worse. Pupils found it difficult to analyse *where* bullying took place, preferring to concentrate on *when*, and that, they felt, was usually beyond the control of teachers — before or after school, at break and lunchtime —confirming the working party's views about the need to provide safe havens for pupils at such times.

The survey, though depressing, gave the working party the evidence they needed: namely that the pupils did not trust the staff's piecemeal interventions and that only a whole-school policy administered in a consistent way would improve matters.

3.3 Launch of the Policy

The policy was well received by staff. At the after-school launch, the Head of Maths went through the survey results. In Year Groups, members of the working party led discussions on the document and its implications for staff. Staff were supportive and suggested only a few changes — mainly to layout. The groups identified issues for future consideration, such as use of tutorial time, more training in survival skills for victims, and creating 'safe havens' for pupils to go to if they felt threatened, and the need to share good classroom practice.

Governors had been kept informed of developments throughout by the Teacher Governor, who was a member of the working party and via written reports. The governors took the same view as the Principal, that is, that the problem existed and that pretending otherwise helped no-one. The response from parents was also supportive. Parents of known bullies were understanding of the school's condemnation of the behaviour and appreciated the school's support of them in their relationships with their children. Parents of victims were naturally delighted that the school was taking such a positive stance. The school's plans were explained directly to parents through the school's newsletter and the brochure distributed to the parents of incoming pupils.

The on-site Carnegie Community Centre, with its full-time members of staff, provides an important link with the local community. With their access to the views of a wide section of the community their support was important. The Centre's philosophies coincide with the views of the working party and its work, especially with pupils from the middle schools and the high school, served to enhance the school initiative. Further ways of including the Carnegie staff in the promotion of the policy are being explored.

The policy fits in with others in school: policies on discipline, equal opportunities, PSE and so on. In some ways drawing together these different strands has been a slow process. Other initiatives have helped to make the atmosphere of the school a more civilised and civilising one. Some £4,000 has been spent on the Carnegie Hall, to provide a comfortable and quiet area for pupils. These changes have been very popular with pupils in Years 9 and 10. One of the benefits of being a community school is access to a full-time member of staff and the facilities of the community centre. That the member of staff is aware of the efforts to combat bullying helps to reinforce the policy.

Other initiatives in school strive towards an atmosphere of respect for and tolerance of others, and for a co-operative, collaborative ethos. The idiosyncratically named 'SAS' group (Survive And Succeed) is looking at how Minsthorpe staff manages the most disruptive pupils, in terms of both the sanctions and the rewards used. The objective is for all pupils to recognise the value of adopting certain types of behaviour. The SAS group and the bullying working party recognise the need for the pupils to 'own' the values and attitudes required to create a positive school ethos. The next step is to 'translate' the policy document produced by adults, into 'pupil speak', written by and for the pupils (see page 110).

3.4 The pyramid

The working party soon recognised that at the age of 13 an individual's patterns of behaviour are already well established. If pupils and parents know that common standards are being set, from nursery school to high school the chances that behaviour will improve are increased. At a meeting of the Headteachers in the pyramid, general support was given to the notion of highlighting bullying as an issue in the schools. In a follow-up discussion with the LEA Pastoral Adviser, the schools declared their willingness to co-operate with the High School.

One of the schools had already moved tentatively towards a policy statement, encouraging pupils to play together in co-operative activities at break and lunchtime. Despite the 4 to 18 age range, the interpretations of bullying and the strategies adopted to counter it were remarkably consistent,

GUIDELINES FOR DEALING WITH A BULLYING INCIDENT.

1.

- Tackling minor incidents will reduce the occurrence of more serious bullying.
- 'Minor' incidents include name-calling; 'looks'; 'borrowing' equipment; spoiling another student's work; pushing in at the dinner queue.

2.

a. Give protection to the victim by:

- moving closer to those involved
- taking some action
- physically separating those involved
- removing either bully or victim, depending on circumstances, away from the scene.

b. Give support to the victim by:

- reassuring the victim that staff can and will help
- comforting the victim
- offering long-term support by training assertiveness; developing coping strategies.

3.

- The bully must be told by the member of staff directly involved that her/his behaviour is unacceptable. Other staff may be involved later eg. taking a class for a few minutes to allow the teacher to deal with the incident.
- Though initial disapproval might be shown in a forceful manner, it is important that at some stage disapproval is expressed in a calm, rational way, ie. avoid bullying the bully.
- In any follow-up work it is vital that possible alternative behaviour is explored. The full range of sanctions is available for specific incidents, though the long-term aim is to help the bully by tackling the underlying problem.

4.

- Students involved as spectators need to know how they can help to create a more pleasant place for all, e.g. by reporting incidents.

5.

- Direct contact is the best, though not always the easiest, method of communication between teacher and tutor. Notes in pigeon holes can be used for back-up.
- The tutor should monitor and review incidents, to get an overall picture of individual students as bullies/victims. Once a tutor becomes aware that a student is giving cause for concern, HoY must be informed.

a very important point not to be overlooked by staff in every school. The advice and comments of the Headteachers of the feeder schools was highly valued and some attended the working party's meetings and also the launch of the Minsthorpe policy. The growth in mutual trust and confidence was reflected in the attendance at a National Conference on bullying by the Educational Psychologist and staff from several schools in the pyramid. Perhaps the greatest achievement of the policy launch day has been that anti-bullying programmes now have an even higher profile, both in the individual schools and the communities served.

As a consequence of this sharing, a further pyramid day is planned for the next academic year, to include a display of pupils' work in a wide range of subject areas, covering the entire age range and involving parents, governors, police, School Psychological Service, Youth Service, and outside speakers. The benefits of marketing the pyramid pro-actively as caring schools should outweigh any doubts raised by a public admission that bullying takes place.

The school has also been involved in the Wakefield Schools Project. This allows schools to identify their areas of need and develop work programmes to satisfy them. A team of twelve staff met with a social worker to plan and evaluate a programme of six sessions. Heads of Year suggested pupils who would benefit most. Parental permission was sought for the programme, aimed at building self-confidence and self esteem in pupils. Each session used groupwork to develop confidence and trust, and to experiment with strategies which the pupils could use in situations requiring them to be assertive. Most of the pupils found the programme worthwhile as it helped them to cope with difficult situations both within and outside the group. The staff involved also found the sessions useful in giving them insights into how the pupils felt and how to use these insights when dealing with other pupils. The methodologies used in the project could be transferred to the classroom, helping staff to recognise and forestall potential problems.

The school also benefited from their contribution to the Psychological Service's monthly meetings. The sessions were initially used to update colleagues on bullying, and the Minsthorpe staff were soon delivering INSET courses to other schools in the area.

3.4 Evaluation

The only objective data gathered by the school were from the initial survey. A follow-up survey is planned to measure the impact of the work. As the awareness of both staff and pupils increased, more bullying became evident than staff had thought. If the number of incidents reported to tutors is anything to go by, the rise was dramatic, particularly following an assembly on the subject. This was at first interpreted by staff as failure but can be construed as positive. If pupils are more willing to tell their teachers about incidents which concern them, then the trend revealed by the survey, namely that the pupils were unwilling to tell teachers, has already been reversed.

Slowly, as staff adopt a more pro-active approach to the problem, they gain the confidence of pupils, which in turn gives pupils the confidence to act on their own. Pupils now show increasing willingness to talk openly about bullying. Two pupils have written and performed their own song about it. Pupils have also responded by creating a more respectful, pleasant, calm and positive working atmosphere. Outside the classroom there are also signs that the pupils are willing to intervene and stop bullying incidents.

Bullying, initially seen as a whole-school matter is now a whole pyramid, or even whole community issue. Any evaluation is therefore problematic. At a school level, the continuing drive to establish set procedures to be adopted by all adults and all pupils is evidence of the effectiveness of the policy. At a community level, the preparations for the community day in July 1993 are testament to the determination of the community to tackle the problem.

4. Millfield School, Street, Somerset

Rev. Tom Wilkinson, Senior Chaplain

Millfield School is an Independent School. It is co-educational for pupils aged 13 to 18, with approximately 1250 pupils, of whom some 900 are boarders, living in 28 boarding houses. Its pupils are drawn from all parts of Britain and the world; some 12% of pupils come from overseas. Thus it is multi-ethnic, multicultural and multi-religious. There are about 160 full-time teachers, each of whom, as a Group tutor, has pastoral responsibility for around 12 pupils. Pastoral care is shared between Houseparents, Heads of Year and Group Tutors. Each pupil is continuously cared for in a small peer group, for three years in the lower school and for two years in the sixth form. At Head of Year level, a three year rotation of oversight in the lower school, with a two year rotation at sixth form level, ensures continuity of contact and care. The vertical house structure for pupils of 13 to 18 years also ensures that pupils who spend five years at Millfield will normally experience continuous house care from Houseparents, Assistant Houseparents and House Liaison Tutors for the whole of their school careers. The same pattern applies to pupils entering the school for two years in the sixth form. Further pastoral care is offered by the school's medical centre, served by two doctors, one male, one female, three nursing sisters and two relief sisters.

Back-up care is provided by the chaplaincy team. A voluntary counselling service has been offered for a number of years by interested staff. This has recently been reinforced by the appointment of a part-time counsellor from outside the school. The counsellor's role includes the regular care of pupils under stress. The counsellor is available for any pupil, at the pupil's initiative, for confidential counselling. The counsellor also provides in-service training for pastoral staff. Before the start of the summer term 1992, a staff development day on many aspects of pastoral care, including the issue of bullying, was led by one of the editors. This was attended by the Headmaster, the Bursar, the Deputy Headmaster, Heads of Year and house staff.

4.1 The beginnings

Constant emphasis on personal welfare and the needs of the individual, undertaken within small groups, has been a hallmark of the school's pastoral care policy. The initiative to engage in the present in-depth review of the school's response to bullying was encouraged by the former Head who ordered copies of the booklet *Bullying: A Positive Response* for all house staff and made the booklet available to all other staff. The need for vigilance and a discussion of bullying in general were treated as high priority in meetings of Heads of Year, Houseparents and staff generally.

The Headmaster, with support from the governing body, discussed the school's approach to bullying at all levels. A school statement has been published, which is discussed with all pupils; it is published on all school and house notice-boards and has been communicated to parents. It now forms part of the school's prospectus and is printed below:

> At Millfield, the importance of caring for one's neighbour is emphasised regularly at every level of staff-pupil contact: for example, in Houses, in assemblies, in tutor groups, through the PSE course discussions and in a hundred other ways which cumulatively comprise the ethos of the school.
>
> Millfield regards the right of every child to enjoy all aspects of his or her education here, without interference from other pupils, as being of paramount importance. Any incident where a pupil's conduct adversely affects another's ability to enjoy this right is deplored. However, when a pupil persistently or repeatedly acts in such a way that another's happiness is directly and seriously affected, we are likely to regard this conduct as bullying. We take such cases very seriously. Pupils are told and regularly reminded that allegations of bullying will always be investigated thoroughly.
>
> When allegations of bullying are proved against a pupil, beyond reasonable doubt, the pupil concerned may be required to leave the school.

Parents and pupils are encouraged to report any signs of bullying they may notice with Houseparents, Group Tutors, Heads of Year, the School Medical Officer, counsellor or any other person, on the clear understanding that such report will be taken seriously and investigated thoroughly. The school generates a community ethos by encouraging pupils to strike up relationships with non-teaching staff, so that cleaners, caretakers, gardeners, coaches, secretarial staff and so on become an integral part of the informal structure of care and service to the pupils. The staff in the medical centre are also fully involved members of the care team. As required by the Children Act, the school's medical officer is officially advertised and appointed as an independent person to whom pupils, parents and staff may report anything which concerns them. They may also turn to the school counsellor.

Open discussion of bullying, with plenty of opportunity to review its occurrence in all areas of school life, is one aspect of a structured programme of Personal, Social and Moral Education (PSME) which operates as a fully integrated part of the school's curriculum. In September 1991 a new Head of PSME was appointed. A weekly teaching period is devoted to aspects of PSME, the Head of Year and the Group Tutors delivering the programme.

In-service training programmes are arranged for staff involved in pastoral care. One such programme, led by one of the editors, addressed the problem of bullying. House prefects and friends are encouraged to watch out and alert staff to signs of bullying. Training programmes for prefects are conducted in houses or at school and guides are appointed to help new pupils; disciplinary action is taken in cases of bullying in consultation with the pupils involved, their parents, Houseparents, Head of Year, the Deputy Headmaster and the Headmaster.

4.2 Further Developments

From within the group of staff offering voluntary, confidential counselling a small working party was set up. It organised a survey of opinion within the intake year of 13 year old pupils (Millfield's third form or Year 9 pupils) during the academic year 1990-91. A questionnaire was organised by the English Department. It was decided to focus on the school's third form as transition between schools is invariably a time of apprehension for many youngsters and bullying is a major fear. About 40% of pupils transfer from Edgarley, our junior preparatory school for about 500 pupils; the rest come from schools in the UK and many countries across the world.

The survey fits into the school's overall concern that young people enjoy their years at Millfield. The questionnaire (see page 120-122) was not scientific so its findings should be interpreted with caution. Open-ended questions were used in order to find out how well third formers settled in — and assess the effectiveness of the support system.

Millfield was alerted to a recently published report, *The Boarding School Line* (La Fontaine and Morris, 1992) which indicates that bullying is the main problem reported by pupils (see Table below). Others included homesickness, parent problems, divorce and bereavement.

Distribution of main problem by gender (La Fontaine and Morris, 1992)				
Main Problems	Female	Male	Total	% Total
Bullying	144	56	200	19.76
Sexual Abuse	80	75	155	15.32
Friendship problem	82	9	91	8.99
Physical Abuse	31	25	56	5.53

The Boarding School Line, jointly funded by the Department of Education and the Independent Schools Joint Committee and operated by the charity ChildLine, ran for six months from January 13th to July 31st, 1991. The line aimed to help children in boarding school and to provide them with confidential counselling and support. A total of 10,315 calls were received. Callers were aged between 12 and 15 years and girls used the line much more than boys, even though boys outnumber girls in boarding schools by almost two to one. Over a third of the calls (35.07%) referred to two main problems: bullying (19.76%) and sexual abuse (15.32%).

Pupils in boarding schools cannot escape after school from those who bully them. So an effective pastoral and counselling programme is important, to encourage children to talk about their worries. According to the special line report, dormitories are a danger zone. The report also found that senior pupils, even monitors and prefects can be the ones threatening and intimidating younger pupils, which is particularly distressing as it leaves victims feeling that there is no safe place in the school.

In the school's survey of its new intake, a high proportion (87%) of the pupils indicated that they had enjoyed their first term at Millfield. Most reported that they had got on well with their House Prefects. This figure was even higher for boarders , of whom only 5% indicated 'poor' relationships. Not surprisingly, 37% of day pupils did not know their House Prefects well enough to answer the question. At the time of the survey (Autumn, 1990) 51% of the pupils were unable to comment about their relationships with School Prefects, since they seldom meet them.

Staff were concerned to learn that 50% of pupils had not found their 'guide' — appointed for each new pupil— to be useful. Third formers (Year 9) usually have a fourth former (Year 10) as a guide. The guide's task is to ensure that new pupils are escorted to meals, lessons, games and so on, and introduced to staff. New pupils can expect to be shown all key areas of the school and generally welcomed and looked after during their first ten to fourteen days in the school. In such a large school with an extensive campus, a good guide can help enormously in the early days of settling in. One youngster wrote, 'If you get a bad guide it ruins your life!'

As a result of the pupils' responses to the questionnaire the school plans to:

■ Look more closely into the selection process for guides.
■ Provide guides with more detailed written guidance and instruction.
■ Devise ways of giving praise and recognition to guides for a 'job well done'.

■ Devise adequate procedures for checking the efficiency of the guiding system by strengthening the report-back arrangements by both guide and new pupil and the Houseparents, on a daily basis.

Encouragingly, 85% of pupils wrote that they were happy all or most of the time. The happiest tended to be either the day pupils or those who had boarded before arriving at Millfield. An important element in enabling new pupils to settle happily into the school is to ensure that they have at least one friend. The following table shows how important adolescents find it to have friends as confidants.

Question 10
Who do you think can help if things are not going well?

First choice	Group Tutor	10.1%
	House Parent	12.6%
	Friend	34.0%
	Parent/Relation	14.2%
	Counsellor	5.7%
	Tutor	5.7%
	No-one	2.4%
	Others (Including Chaplain, Head of Year, Senior Pupils)	5.2%
	Don't Know	10.1%

The purpose of the question was to see where pupils felt they could turn for help and their replies need to be interpreted carefully. The responses were no doubt influenced by the type of problem they had in mind as they answered the question — which we cannot know. Answers to other questions would suggest that Millfield is relatively free of serious problems. If the pupils were thinking of the everyday problems that beset all adolescents, it is probably appropriate that a large number of pupils stated that their friends were best placed to help them.

National research indicates that in a boarding community, some seek to dominate others and new, junior pupils are most vulnerable. They may be subjected to initiation rituals and general harassment by older and stronger pupils. Research also indicates that school transfer is a peak period for being bullied and that the frequency of self-reported bullying declines with age (Olweus, 1989). This may be explained by the fact that senior pupils have fewer peers who are bigger and stronger but, more importantly, that youngsters learn alternative social skills which enable them to cope with aggression and threats as they mature.

Using open-ended questions enabled the school to ask pupils, 'What do you think is meant by bullying?' (Question 13a). It is interesting to observe that many held wider perceptions of bullying behaviour than is recognised by adults — including teachers. Here are a selection of their views:

- *Bullying is when a person or persons continually either emotionally or physically to harass another pupil.*
- *The verbal or physical abuse of (usually) a younger child by those in a superior position to them.*
- *Girls usually verbal bully towards each other which can be more hurtful. Boys fight each other — physical.*
- *Verbal or physical abuse, like being racist, teasing them if they are fat or have spots. Bothering them constantly.*
- *Calling people names in a fashion other than casual joking (even that can be bullying if done excessively) and physically harming them. In general doing anything that makes someone else unhappy.*

In the light of what had already emerged, these comments were hardly surprising. Staff were greatly concerned that many third formers reported being bullied — three in ten said they felt they had been bullied and one in ten admitted to having bullied someone. From the responses it is not possible to determine whether some of the incidents were just 'one off', nor who had been involved, nor the nature of the bullying. The school's findings compare with the age pattern of pupils who used the Boarding School Line. Although the ChildLine Survey did not have a scientifically selected sample, it reported that the greater proportion of callers were aged 13 — some 20% of the total. It is reassuring that staff at Millfield had detected the problems before the information became available from ChildLine and acted to limit the problems that pupils in the school experience.

In their report, the authors of the Boarding School Line write:

> ChildLine's experience with a special line for those being bullied is that children's definition of this term is very wide and this is confirmed by the reports of bullying given by boarding school pupils. Teasing, particularly persistent teasing which the victims cannot stop, is understood in the same terms as beatings and violence; it is hostile behaviour that excludes the bullied child from the group, causes pain and undermines his or her self-esteem. Many of the callers were suffering from teasing that ridiculed their appearance, their accents, their possessions or the wealth or class of their parents. Almost any characteristic was used as the pretext for ridicule. Children commonly said that they were being teased for being fat, for not wearing the clothes or shoes thought appropriate by others, or by being different in some way from their

peers. In some cases, the teasing was the manifestation of local, national or racial prejudice, as for example when an Indian child reported that he was bullied because he was black. The victims of bullying felt isolated and humiliated; several reported that it interfered with their school work. The most despairing might run away or have thoughts of suicide (La Fontaine and Morris 1992).

4.3 Evaluation

All pupils are aware of the school's attitude to bullying and so are parents and staff. The house staff have become more aware of the increasing openness which the issue receives in the reviewing and planning of pastoral care within the school. The programme to counter bullying has positively influenced the school's awareness of the issues involved in making judgements about what bullying means to pupils; the need for vigilance by everyone, both children and adults; the need to counsel, support and guide those who at times seem to seek victimisation, as well as those who indulge in bullying behaviour.

Attention has been paid to staggering meal times and providing places of safety and quiet, as was done at Minsthorpe. In September 1992, a third form centre was opened, where new pupils and others can meet their peers and share in activities appropriate to their age group, or simply relax in peace.

Pupils now understand the seriousness with which bullying is viewed. Although it is difficult to quantify, much more support appears to be forthcoming from the pupils themselves than was true before the staff intervened and deliberate statements about tackling bullying were publicised.

A side issue has been the dilemma for prefects: if they act firmly, might they be accused of intimidating pupils? The more manipulative younger pupils have become 'wise' to the levels of protection offered to them and tend to push their luck with prefects and even staff! Nevertheless, the issue of bullying and ways of dealing with the problem has become a lively concern for all members of the school community.

Appendix
STRICTLY CONFIDENTIAL
Introduction

1. The purpose of this questionnaire is to see how you, as a third year pupil, have settled into life at Millfield. We hope this will also help future third year pupils.

2. Please try to answer all the questions as honestly and fully as possible.

3. Your replies will be treated in the strictest confidence. Therefore, we do not need to know your name, group or house.

4. We will, of course, look very carefully at everything you write. However, it will take a long time to analyse all your answers, so do not expect any immediate feedback.

5. Thank you very much for your help.

1. It will be useful to know a little information about you, but it will not be possible to identify you. Please tick the appropriate boxes.

   Are you: male ☐   female ☐

   boarder ☐   day ☐

   from Edgarley ☐   from another school ☐

   in-house ☐   out-house ☐

   Is this your first year at Millfield?   Yes ☐ No ☐

   Have you boarded before?   Yes ☐ No ☐

2. How much did you enjoy your first term at Millfield? Say why.

3. Are there things you dislike about Millfield? If so, what are they?

4. (a) How well do you get on with your house prefects?

 (b) How well do you get on with school prefects?

 (c) How well do you get on with other older pupils?

5. How well did your guide help you settle in?

6. If there were things you could change about life at Millfield, what would they be?

7. For most of the time would you say you were happy at school? Circle one of the following which best describes how you feel.

 Happy — all the time   Unhappy — some of the time

 — most of the time   — most of the time

 — some of the time   — some of the time

 — never   — never

8. (a) Are there any times and places you feel happy?

 (b) Are there any times and places you feel unhappy?

9. Have you come across pupils who are unhappy? Without giving names, would you say why?

10. Who do you think can help you if things are not going well?

11. How do you feel about the way Millfield pupils treat each other?

12. (a) Have you ever seen anyone made very unhappy by another pupil?

   (b) What do you think made them unhappy?

13. (a) What do you think is meant by bullying?

   (b) Since arriving at Millfield have you seen anyone being bullied?

   (c) Since arriving at Millfield have you been bullied?

   (d) Since arriving at Millfield have you bullied anyone?

14. Is there anything else you would like to add about life at Millfield?

Your houseparent or group tutor, or any of the counselling team, would be pleased to help if you would like to talk about some of your answers with someone.

Theme Four

Educational and Other Agencies

Introduction

In the previous themes, we have seen how staff in schools, along with their governing bodies, pupils and parents, can counter bullying through management techniques, the development of curriculum materials and concentration on the transitional years. In this section, we look at how outside agencies, both advisory and supportive, can provide valuable links with home and the wider community and thereby help schools to deal with bullying.

These agencies can include advisers, inspectors, support agencies like the Educational Welfare Service and the Educational Psychological Service, in-service trainers and other organisations, such as the Gulbenkian Foundation and pressure groups like the Anti-Bullying Campaign (ABC). Each has a role to play to raise awareness and increase understanding and to work out different strategies and approaches.

At Beaumont Leys, the staff were stimulated by the timely intervention of the Educational Welfare Officer. The school must be commended, for it was one of the first schools to tackle bullying head-on, when many others were unwilling to do so for fear of presenting a negative image. The school is one of the first to have both a 'before' and 'after' questionnaire which can easily be used by other schools; it is a model of its kind.

At Cardinal Newman R.C. School the co-ordinator of special needs became involved with the project along with the Educational Welfare Officer, since it was apparent that a number of pupils were being disentitled. The school draws from a wide and varied catchment area, as it serves all the Catholic primary schools in Luton. There is a large Irish community who are often the butt of racist jokes and nicknames, such as 'Mick', or 'Spud', or 'Paddy' and so on. Such name-calling of ethnic and cultural minorities is, of course, a form of racial abuse. This school tackled the problems in a holistic way.

At Woodside, we can see how bullying can be tackled alongside other issues like home-school relations. Of all the forms of anti-social behaviour, bullying brings the home and school into greatest conflict through mistrust, disagreement, accusation and counter-accusation. Many parents report that schools are unsympathetic and end up 'blaming the victim' by transferring the pupil to another group or even institution. This, of course, is a non-solution since the ethos of the school is not changed and the bullying continues. Woodside tried to address these problems with the help of the Local Authority's adviser.

The Quaker Peace Education Project shows how pupils can find their own solutions to the problems which beset them, providing that they are supported. It is surprising that Local Education Authorities have not become more pro-active in dealing with the problem of bullying. This project in Ulster shows the depth of talent that pupils can bring to bear upon the subject, how creative they can be and how easily the lessons learned can be transferred into schools.

1. Beaumont Leys School, Leicester

Sue Eley, Deputy Headteacher
Barbara Blatherwick, Education Welfare Officer

Beaumont Leys is a well established comprehensive school catering for pupils in the 11-19 age range. It is situated on the northern outskirts of the city of Leicester. The school was originally opened in 1957 as a mixed secondary modern school. It was enlarged to cater for the then growing school population and was reorganised as a comprehensive school in 1974. By 1981 there were over 1600 pupils on roll but this fell during the subsequent decade to 700. Numbers are rising once more and the school expects to have 800 on roll shortly.

The school is situated in an open site of approximately 15 acres. It serves a catchment area which provides a mixture of privately owned and council owned housing, serving white collar, skilled and semi-skilled groups. Thus pupils come from widely differing homes and cultural backgrounds. A significant number of pupils come, or have parents who come, from the Indian subcontinent — about 18%. There are smaller numbers of Chinese, Vietnamese and others of Afro-Caribbean origin. The school is fed by more than eight primary schools, five of which can be classified as the main feeder schools.

1.1 The beginnings

A chance remark by a tutor to the Educational Welfare Officer (EWO) proved to be the catalyst for the campaign to counter bullying in the school. It took the EWO about eighteen months to reach the conclusion that bullying was a considerable factor in non-attendance at school. Since there was no school policy on bullying, there was no consistent response from the school. The degree to which a pupil was helped and supported was a matter of luck. The EWO realised that many staff took the problem seriously but they were not necessarily accessible to all pupils, many of whom were suffering in silence.

The day the remark was made the EWO had been to visit a serious non-attender, a bright girl of thirteen who had transferred from another school and who could not sustain more than a few days' attendance at a time. Her mother supported her absences and the excuses given were clearly fabricated. Finally, after many months of visiting, the girl broke down and disclosed that she was being bullied. Although she tried her best to come to school and had no problem coping with her lessons, she could not face the classmates who would not talk to her but talked about her, who would not sit next to her or include her in any activity.

With this new knowledge and confident that she now knew the real reason for the absences, the EWO approached the tutor who, she was sure, was best placed to help the girl. The tutor's response was dismissive, however: 'It's her own fault. She doesn't try to mix.' It was this comment which decided the EWO to raise the issue with the Senior Management Team.

In a climate of schools being in ever increasing competition with each other, the EWO was concerned that the school would be reluctant to raise an issue with such negative connotations as bullying. However, at the time bullying was receiving considerable media attention. With this media focus, the EWO felt more confident and initially approached one of the Deputy Headteachers who had oversight of the school's anti-racist and anti-sexist policies. Both agreed that bullying was an aspect of equal opportunities issues.

To raise awareness among the staff it was necessary to provide facts and figures pertinent to the problem in their school and to give pupils an opportunity to voice their feelings and opinions. A questionnaire which allowed pupils to tick boxes or give short comments seemed to be the best way of meeting both these requirements. Proposals for such a school wide survey were put to and accepted by the Senior Management Team. During the last week of the Spring term 1991 the pupils completed a questionnaire which explored pupils' experiences of bullying as well as their perceptions of the school's attitudes towards it. An indication of how seriously the pupils took the questionnaire was that only four of them were spoiled — 2% of the total.

The results of the survey showed that bullying was affecting the lives of 19% of all students, with significantly more than that in the lower school, 13% as victims and 6% as bullies. Furthermore, 33% claimed that bullying had at some time made them want to stay away from school and 13% actually having done so. Perhaps the most disturbing point from the school's point of view was that only 50% of pupils thought that the school took bullying seriously. The message came through strongly, reflected in an 80% positive response and the pupils' assertions that they wanted to know that there was someone to go to who would listen to them. It is not surprising that these figures reinforce Reid's findings (1988) that many persistent absentees from school begin their absenteeism as a result of bullying.

BULLYING LINE

You may have noticed recently that a new helpline has been set up for children who may be involved in bullying - either as victims or bullies.

We would like to know your experiences and feelings about this subject, and so we are asking you to take part in this survey.

You may answer questions as briefly as you wish. You can either just tick the boxes or you can add more than we are asking - it's totally up to you.

SECTION 1 - ABOUT YOU

1)   Girl ☐   Boy ☐

2)   1st Year ☐   Age 11 ☐   12 ☐

     2nd " ☐   " 12 ☐   13 ☐

     3rd " ☐   " 13 ☐   14 ☐

     4th " ☐   " 14 ☐   15 ☐

     5th " ☐   " 15 ☐   16 ☐

     Lwr.6th ☐   " 16 ☐   17 ☐

     Uppr.6th ☐   " 17 ☐   18 ☐

3)   U.K./Irish ☐   _____

     Mixed Race ☐   _____

     Asian ☐   _____

     Afro-Caribbean ☐   _____

     Chinese/Vietnamese ☐   _____

     Other ☐   _____

4)   Only Child ☐   _____

     1-3 children in family ☐   _____

     4-6 " " " ☐   _____

     More than 6 children in family ☐   _____

     Eldest ☐   Youngest ☐   _____

BULLYING LINE

5) Do you have a best friend?

   Yes ☐   No ☐

   Do you have lots of friends?

   Yes ☐   No ☐

SECTION 2 - BULLYING

Bullying does not just mean physically hurting someone. There are many forms of bullying. The result is always the same - your life is made a misery.

1) Have you ever been bullied?

   Yes ☐   No ☐

2) Are you bullied now?

   Yes ☐   No ☐

3) Have you been bullied over a long period of time?

   Yes ☐   No ☐

If the answer to all the above questions is NO then you do not need to go any further in this section

4) Are/were you bullied by

   1 or 2 people   ☐

   A gang of people   ☐

   Lots of separate people ☐

5) How long have you been/were you bullied:

   less than 6 months   ☐

   6 months   ☐

   1 - 2 years   ☐

   3 - 4 years   ☐

   longer?   ☐

6) Are/were they children younger than you. ☐

   Children of your age   ☐

   Children older than you ☐

   Adults?   ☐

BULLYING LINE

7) How are/were you bullied?

Did they   hit you ☐ _____

            call you names ☐ _____

            ignore you ☐ _____

            ask you for money? ☐ _____

8) Does/did the bullying take place

        in class ☐ _____

        at break/lunchtimes ☐ _____

        after school ☐ _____

        all the time? ☐ _____

9) Why do you think you are/were bullied?

race ☐ _____

height: shorter ☐ taller ☐ than average _____

size : thinner ☐ larger ☐ than average _____

shyness ☐   hair colour or style ☐ _____

glasses ☐   other features ☐ _____

disabilities ☐   clothes ☐ _____

cleverer ☐ slower ☐ than average _____

other reasons ☐ _____

SECTION 3 - <u>WHAT TO DO</u>

1) Have you/did you tell anyone about the bullying?

      Yes ☐   No ☐ _____

2) If NO why?   You were afraid ☐ _____

             thought no one would listen ☐

             didn't/don't know who to tell ☐

3(a) If YES who?   Parent ☐ _____

               relative ☐ _____

               teacher ☐ _____

               friend ☐ _____

               school counsellor ☐ _____

               other ☐ _____

BULLYING LINE

3(b) What happened?   nothing   ☐

bullying was stopped   ☐

bullying made worse   ☐

bullying stopped for a while   ☐
but then continued.

4) Do you think that the school takes bullying seriously

Yes ☐   No ☐

5) Has bullying ever made you not want to come to school?

Yes ☐   No ☐

6(a) Have you ever stayed away from school to avoid bullying?

Yes ☐   No ☐

(b) If YES did you parents know?   Yes ☐   No ☐

7(a) Do you think there should be one person in school whom you could go to
about bullying?

Yes ☐   No ☐

(b) Should this be a teacher   ☐   or other adult   ☐

(c) Would you choose to talk to a man   ☐   or a woman ☐

SECTION 4 - BULLIES

Remember Bullying does not just mean physically hurting someone.
Anyone that makes another person's life a misery and enjoys doing it
is a Bully.

1) Have you ever been a bully yourself?   Yes ☐   No ☐

2) Are you still a bully?   Yes ☐   No ☐

3) Do/did you ever feel sorry for the person you bully? Yes ☐   No ☐

4(a) Are you/have you ever been part of a gang that bullies someone?

Yes ☐   No ☐

(b) If YES do you/have you joined in   Yes ☐   No ☐

just watched? Yes ☐   No ☐

_____

_____

_____

_____

BULLYING LINE

4(c) Have you wanted to help the person being bullied?

Yes ☐   No ☐

5) Have you bullied other people because someone once bullied you?

Yes ☐   No ☐

6) Have you bullied other people because you enjoy feeling powerful?

Yes ☐   No ☐

7) Have you wanted to stop being a bully?

Yes ☐   No ☐

If YES would you like to talk to someone who would understand and
not blame you?

Yes ☐   No ☐

Would you like to make any other comments?

_____

_____

_____

_____

_____

Thank you for completing this survey. It will help us to discover how important
a problem bullying is to you, and what we can do to stop it.

Don't forget, it is completely anonymous. We will not know who you are unless
you want us to. If you do, just write your name at the top of Page one.

CHILDLINE - 0800 1111

1.2 The school's response

The data obtained from the survey suggested that prompt action was needed. Two staff workshops were held. The first was to raise staff awareness of the issue, particularly as it affected the daily lives of the pupils in the school, to explode some of the myths surrounding bullying and to reach a consensus about what constituted bullying. From this workshop came the agreement that the school needed to develop both policy and practice to counter bullying.

A second workshop was convened shortly afterwards and a draft policy statement outlined. Suggestions were also put forward for strategies which might counteract bullying. At this stage it was felt that a smaller working party was needed to look at this in more detail. The remit of this group was to include some basic assumptions:

1. Bullying is a form of abuse. Like all abuse it is based on power. In the case of bullying the power may not at first be evident; it is assumed by or conceded to those who bully.

2. Pupils have a right to a safe and comfortable place in which to learn. They have an entitlement to equal access to the curriculum. They will not be accorded this if they are absent through fear. If present in school they will not be accorded equal access to the curriculum if they are in fear whilst they are there. Pupils cannot learn if they are in fear or are so undermined as to have little or no confidence left. Bullying is an equal opportunities issue.

3. All staff in the institution are responsible for countering bullying. No-one can avoid the pastoral role; it is integral to what people are and do as workers in a school. There must be a whole-school recognition that bullying is unacceptable and a willingness on the part of all staff to act to reduce it.

4. If we ignore bullying we are colluding with the bullies and allowing it to continue. There are two types of schools: those that admit that it happens and do something about it, and those that deny its existence and so allow it to continue.

Over the next half-term this small group met regularly and drew up a policy statement with suggestions on how to implement the policy. From the outset they agreed to focus on two forms of practical approach: first to devise preventative strategies and secondly determine consistent ways of reacting to occurences of bullying. The policy statement was as follows:

Beaumont Leys School Anti-Bullying Policy Statement

At Beaumont Leys School bullying is defined as:

The repeated intimidation, humiliation and abuse of an individual by one or more other people.

Bullying may be physical, verbal or psychological. It can take the form of:

- *Name-calling*
- *Extortion of money or property*
- *Mental cruelty*
- *'Sending someone to Coventry'*
- *Physical assault*
- *Harassment*
- *Malicious gossip*
- *Forcing people to do things against their will*

The school will not tolerate bullying in any form and will support any student who is subjected to it. Staff will work with pupils who do bully, to enable them to modify their behaviour.

1.3 Implementing the Policy

At this stage the policy was taken to year 7 pupils for their consideration in PSE lessons. They produced a rewording of the policy statement which is now included in the school's induction booklet.

Bullying includes

- *Making a fool of someone*
- *Saying things behind someone's back*
- *Spreading rumours and stories about someone*
- *Name-calling*
- *Taxing (demanding money)*
- *Hitting and kicking someone*
- *Making someone feel small*
- *Damaging someone's property*
- *Making someone do things they don't want to do*
- *Ignoring someone*
- *Nasty looks/staring at someone*
- *Making fun of someone if they have a problem*
- *Picking on someone*
- *Leaving someone out*

- *Deliberately making someone feel scared*
- *Making fun of someone's family*
- *Making fun of where and how someone lives*

Beaumont Leys School will not stand for bullying of any kind. The staff will help anyone who is being bullied. We will also work with people who bully to help them behave better.

The induction booklet is given to all year 6 primary school pupils when they spend three days at Beaumont Leys in June before they join the school in August The policy and practice are also explained to, and discussed by, the pupils as part of their induction programme. In particular they are advised where they can go to seek support if they should be bullied and told what the school regards as bullying.

From this point, ways of broadening the scope of the work were considered so that it could become an integral part of school life. Discussion of bullying and its prevention have been incorporated into the PSE programme in a unit called 'Relationships'. It was felt important to treat bullying in this way rather than isolate it from the wider context in which human relationships occur and are considered.

Staff training was also necessary. One of the aspects of the School Development Plan over a three year cycle was the 'Role of the Tutor'. Staff consensus was reached about the nature of the development plan, so there was a high degree of commitment to developing the tutor's role. The remit for the role of the tutor is a broad one, including the development of counselling skills, increased awareness of the catchment area, anti-bullying work, the development of tutorial and PSE resources and developing strategies for staff support.

As increasing numbers of pupils were coming forward to discuss being bullied, the need for staff to be trained in basic counselling skills was highlighted. A training session was held for the staff, focusing on skills such as active listening, paraphrasing, reflecting and so on. There was discussion about what constituted counselling and how this differed from other forms of equally valid helping, such as offering advice, intervening, taking positive action. Many other issues and problems were aired in addition to bullying.

The induction programme for all new staff, including probationary teachers, was revised to include anti-bullying training. There is now a commitment to this being part of staff induction, since it is important to avoid anti-bullying training being regarded as a 'one off' event. The commitment is to anti-bullying work continuing and being reviewed as new staff join the school, so that they feel part of the process and feel a sense of ownership of the school's policies and practices. Anti-bullying training is also part of the school experience for student teachers. This has been particularly effective with PGCE students who are with the school for an extended period as part of the partnership scheme the school has with the University of Leicester School of Education.

To maintain momentum and further involve the pupils, the proposed responses to bullying were discussed at Student Council. This group consists of two representatives from each year group from years 7-13. Their suggestions were taken into account, especially with regard to disseminating information about the anti-bullying policy and the proposed practices. They have been particularly interested in looking at ways in which pupils could support others who are being bullied.

For many years the school has used homework diaries for the lower school pupils (year 7-9) and coursework diaries for the upper school pupils (10-11). After consultation with the pupils it was decided to revise the format of these so that they became a kind of personal organiser for each person. These were designed together with the Year Heads and now contain a wider range of information than before, including the school's code of conduct, its anti-racist and anti-sexist statement and the anti-bullying policy. These were available at the start of the academic year so that form tutors could use them as an initial stimulus with their tutor groups at the start of the new school year. At the same time the school publicised the fact that a variety of materials was available which gave the pupils concrete examples of what they could do to help stop bullying.

Two bullying referral forms have been designed and distributed. One is for pupil use and enables pupils who may be reluctant to report directly to an adult that they are being bullied or that they have witnessed bullying incidents. Supplies of these slips are kept in prominent areas of the school, including the library, the school office, the Special Needs Department and with form tutors. Completed forms can be posted in a box close to the school office. The box is checked daily. Obviously such a system is open to abuse but few false allegations or invented incidents have been received. The pupils appear to have responded positively to a system which is designed to help them. A second form for staff to complete enables the incidence of bullying to be monitored and is completed on the witnessing or disclosure of an incident. Forms are filed centrally and monitored regularly. This system enables the school to highlight the following information:

Who is involved in the behaviour; these pupils need to be helped.

What form the behaviour is taking.

When the behaviour is taking place so that staff can be especially vigilant at these times.

Where the behaviour is taking place so that the area can be improved or monitored more effectively.

RESULTS OF BULLYING SURVEY/EVALUATION: JANUARY 1992

1. Have you seen the School's anti-bullying policy and procedures?
    YES: 67% NO: 33%

2. Has a teacher gone over the School's anti-bullying policy and procedures with you?
    YES: 67% NO: 33%

3. What colour are the bullying report slips?
    CORRECT: 91% WRONG/DON'T KNOW: 9%

4. Do you know where you could get hold of a bullying report slip?
    YES: 88% NO: 12%

5. Have you been bullied this school year?
    YES: 16% NO: 84%

FOR STUDENTS WHO HAD BEEN BULLIED:

6a Did you use a bullying report slip?
    YES: 16% NO: 84%

6b If you did not use a bullying report slip, did you tell anyone you were being bullied?
    NO: 10% YES: 90%

I told: a teacher	58%
Educational Welfare Officer	21%
friends	62%
parent(s)	46%
someone else	11%

N.B. Several students told more than one group of people that they were being bullied.

6c When you reported that you were being bullied, were you taken seriously?
    YES: 47% NO: 27% NO COMMENT: 26%

6d When you reported that you were being bullied, was anything done about it?
    YES: 48% NO: 26% NO COMMENT: 26%

6e Were you satisfied with what was done?
    YES: 45% NO: 29% NO COMMENT: 26%

6f Would you report it again if you were bullied again?
    YES: 66% NO: 22% NO COMMENT: 12%

RESULTS OF BULLYING SURVEY/EVALUATION: JANUARY 1992 (continued)

FOR STUDENTS WHO HAD NOT BEEN BULLIED:

7a If someone did bully you, would you use a bullying report slip?
YES: 53% NO: 47%

7b If you would not use a bullying report slip, would you tell someone?
YES: 97% NO: 3%

7c If you would tell someone, who would it be?

a teacher	31%
Educational Welfare Officer	3%
friends	53%
parent(s)	47%
other	7%

N.B: Several students said that they would tell more than one group of people, if they were bullied.

YEAR 8 AND 9 STUDENTS ONLY

8. Do you think that the School's action on bullying has improved this year?

ALL STUDENTS:
YES: 47% NO: 42%
DON'T KNOW/NO COMMENT: 11%

BULLIED STUDENTS:
YES: 42% NO: 39%
DON'T KNOW/NO COMMENT: 19%

NOT-BULLIED STUDENTS:
YES: 48% NO: 43%
DON'T KNOW/NO COMMENT: 9%

1.4 Evaluation

With the preventative and short-term measures securely in place, a further questionnaire was administered to the lower school pupils. The lower school was chosen since it was here that the figures had been high in the initial survey so it had been a target group for the process described above. The aim was to see if the pupils thought the new procedures were effective and supported them. Predictably the results of the survey brought a mixed reaction.

There was some disappointment that only 47% of pupils thought that the school's actions on countering bullying had improved matters over the year. However, the school can take heart from the fact that nearly half of the pupils in the lower school felt that the situation in school had improved concerning bullying. No-one said that the situation had worsened.

This had been achieved only 100 days after the introduction of the procedures! Of further encouragement was the fact that so many pupils were aware of the school's anti-bullying policy and procedures. On a qualitative level, things feel better around the school and staff are aware of pupils speaking out more. Pupils appear to be developing the expectation that they will not be bullied, or that if they are, they have the right to know that something will be done about it.

Currently the school is looking to tie its anti-bullying policy more closely to other aspects of its equal opportunities work. A coherent picture needs to emerge. However, whether anti-bullying work will be additional to equal opportunities work or an integral part of it remains to be seen. Clearly racism is one motive for bullying but not all racism is necessarily bullying. Particular racist incidents must of course be challenged and dealt with alongside the preventative work of the school, but to tie this work to that of bullying, as yet, remains problematic.

Further attention needs to be given to the increased involvement and training of support staff, although initial moves have been made in this direction. The school needs to raise the awareness of parents, governors and the wider community about its anti-bullying policy and procedures and to examine ways of encouraging their active participation in helping the school realise its objectives. Major targets are the assurance that bullying will be taken seriously and that something will be done about it. This will achieve another step in breaking down the levels of secrecy among pupils in which bullying thrives. The school needs to examine ways by which its atmosphere is made even more conducive to encouraging pupils to talk to adults about things which concern them, including bullying. The hope is that these measures will make the policy and procedures for countering bullying real to all those involved in the life of the school, and that they will have ownership of these systems and values. For the essential aim is the improvement of the school environment for *all* who work in it.

This process would not be complete without one final anecdote which is testimony to the efforts of all those involved in the development of the anti-bullying policy and procedures at Beaumont Leys School. The bullied girl whose plight had set things in motion was successfully helped through her problems. She is now a happy sixteen year old with a steady set of friends and the prospect of achieving good grades in a wide range of GCSE courses. Last term she was awarded a certificate for 100% attendance.

2. Cardinal Newman R.C. School, Luton

Linda Hardman, Co-ordinator of Special Needs and Curriculum Support

Another example of the effective work of support agencies can be seen in this example from Cardinal Newman Roman Catholic School, Luton. The school is situated on the northern borders of Luton in a pleasant semi-rural location. It is the only Roman Catholic Secondary school in Luton and is over subscribed. Luton is a cosmopolitan community, housing people from a variety of cultural backgrounds. There are approximately 1,250 pupils on roll from years 7-13. Luton has a large Irish community and many of these children attend the school

2.1 The beginnings

In her role of co-ordinating the special educational needs of pupils, the Head of Curriculum Support works closely with the Educational Support Services, liaising with them in a positive, preventative way. After consultation with the EWO bullying became a priority on their agenda as it can, as we have already seen, disentitle some pupils from the curriculum and is a major factor in cases of non-attendance. At a meeting with the Educational Psychologist they were made aware of the work of the Neti- Neti Theatre Company (1990) and the booklet *Bullying: A Positive Response* The EP also provided them with a copy of a questionnaire devised and used by the Luton team of EPs in another local school. The questionnaire was designed specifically for younger pupils, but the ideas were helpful and could be adapted for an older age group.

The initiative was further developed when the Head of Curriculum Support was invited to deliver an assembly and saw it as an ideal opportunity to address the issue with the whole school. Using materials from the booklet, selecting different extracts to target different age groups and adding a religious dimension with Saul's Conversion in Acts 9, the assemblies were well received, triggering positive comments from staff and pupils alike. This was an effective springboard. Awareness had been raised and both staff and pupils were receptive to developing initiatives in school. The Head of Curriculum Support met with the Deputy Headteacher in charge of pastoral welfare in the school and together they developed a plan of action. The timescale was tight, but was generally adhered to:

Week 1: Present bullying as the main item on the agenda at a Head of House meeting.

Week 2: Explain the initiative to year 7 pupils.

Week 3: During PSE half the year 7 cohort complete the questionnaire.

Week 4: During PSE the other half of the cohort complete the questionnaire. Special Needs Co-ordinator collates responses.

Week 5: Feedback responses to Heads of Houses.

Week 6: Feedback responses to pupils.

The long-term aim was to encourage staff to develop a positive approach to the problem of bullying in school and, as at Beaumont Leys, to provide information that could raise staff awareness of the problem.

2.2 Further developments

To ensure that the questionnaire was completed by all Year 7 pupils, the support and co-operation of the Heads of House, other House staff and Year 7 tutors was needed. To secure that support, the following points were raised at the Heads of House meeting:

1. Pastoral staff in all schools spend a great deal of time and energy dealing with the consequences of bullying; counselling victims and bullies, informing parents and sometimes seeking advice from outside agencies. Working as a team on preventative methods of coping with bullying would be a better strategy than the time-consuming reactive methods in current use. Building an assertiveness training programme into the delivery of PSE was one strategy suggested.

2. Children have a right to receive their education free from abuse and humiliation. It is the responsibility of teachers, pastoral staff in particular, to ensure that this takes place in an atmosphere which is caring and protective.

3. The school's supportive pastoral structure could enable the school to lead the way for other schools in the area in the positive management of pupil behaviour.

The pastoral heads were receptive to these ideas and supportive of any ideas which developed positive pupil relationships. They were anxious to ensure that the school focused on the positive dimensions of the initiative, as they did not want parents and prospective parents to think that bullying was a big problem at Cardinal Newman School. Therefore it was decided to inform parents of the developments through the Parents' Newsletter in the following way:

Cardinal Newman School has been invited to contribute to a 'good practice' project on bullying in school by the Cardiff Institute of Higher Education. We are one of eight secondary schools nationally who are taking part.

The project will involve issuing a questionnaire to all year 7 pupils during PSE. The pupils will be invited to return an anonymous response to ensure complete honesty in their disclosures.

The pastoral staff led by our Head of Curriculum Support will analyse the responses and devise strategies, plans and a policy for developing a preventative approach to bullying.

The Cardiff Institute of Higher Education is looking to schools like ours with its supportive pastoral structure to lead the way for other schools in the positive management of bullying.

This is just one way of reassuring parents and helping to put initiatives such as this in context, not only for the staff but also for parents and the community generally. Finally, guidelines were given to staff about the completion of the questionnaire and it was administered on the appointed date.

2.3 The responses.

Collating the responses was an onerous task, in this case carried out by a single person. It would have been beneficial to have used a grid format, as in the one at Beaumont Leys, and to have gathered support for its collation. Nevertheless, the responses were informative, helpful and illuminating:

Why do some pupils get 'picked on'?

'There is something different about them... dress sense... cheeky... physical attributes... they act scared... they have expensive briefcases for carrying expensive equipment... brainy... they have lots of merit marks... wear glasses... handicapped/disabled in some way... slow learners... teacher's pet... colour... accent... financially poor.'
All of these will be familiar to teachers, but it underlines the insights which pupils have into the problem.

Where does bullying take place?

'In corners... out of sight of the teachers... in the playground... in places where teachers don't go... in the toilets... at the back of the gym... on the buses... behind the huts... on the back road by the bike sheds... when walking home... in class when the teacher isn't looking or listening...'

Again there is nothing surprising about the responses, but they point to the need for greater vigilance by staff.

Can teachers do anything about bullying?

'No! Teachers rarely take bullying seriously... they do not fully understand... they can make matters worse... bullies won't listen — they are uncontrollable... the bully will bully you even more... they cannot do anything... it's difficult for them to intervene in incidents which happen outside the schoolgrounds... the victim has to sort it out.'

To be faced with those kinds of responses from youngsters is saddening for anyone involved in teaching. It also told the staff at Cardinal Newman that there was an urgent need to tackle the problem.

2.4 Action plans

Ideas from the booklet *Bullying: A Positive Response'* were then posited as a way forward in the positive management of bullying. Since this is a Catholic school, it was felt that the School Chaplain may have a role to play

142

in presenting a sympathetic, listening ear to the pupils. There is a well organised programme of Personal and Social Education at the school as well as an extensive RE programme. Pupils also follow a Complementary Studies course in Years 10 and 11 which augments the PSE and RE courses. Therefore, a wide variety of curricular materials is available to promote consistent values. Some of the stimuli available in the English Department further reinforces these values. This has led to a number of exciting developments with the pupils' work. Posters have been designed and displayed around the school.

BULLYING

If one of my friends was being bullied it would be a serious thing. Bullying is not fun- it's something which is horrible and can hurt people bably. So if one of my friend or just someone I knew was getting picked on, I would have you report it to someone I could trust to help this person, or a tutor or or even a parent. I would do this because I think every child in High School has a responsibilaty to thier friends to help them when they are in need

If a friend or someone I did not knew very well was getting bullied maybe I would tell someone or I would go over to help them. Now to help them, I mean to go over and tell the bully to go away, or to quickly tell a teacher who would have a quick response to this. In High school you have a responsabilaty to help not just a friend even if this person is an enemy. Help them dont just tell a teacher also help HELP THEM.

Written work has also been developed, giving advice and offering insights into the nature of bullying. Poetry can be an effective stimulus too, even for the less able pupil.

To draw these differing threads together it was decided to make the issue part of the whole school development plan. The pastoral teams chose 'Pupil Relationships' (including an anti-bullying campaign) as their priority. The targets were:

- To encourage pupils to be more caring and thoughtful to each other.
- To remove fear, intimidation and bullying as far as possible.
- To enhance the reputation of the school in the town as one with a caring atmosphere.

To achieve these targets, the following tasks needed to be done:

1. Questionnaire administered to *all* pupils by *all* tutors.
2. A recording system of bullying incidents to be set up and monitored by the pastoral heads.

BULLIES

Bullies are bad
They can drive you mad.
If you watch them.
You are just as bad.

Bullying will happen
Unless you make it stop
They will do things even worse
If you let it go on.

---

3. House assemblies given to raise awareness of the problems associated with bullying and to stress the importance of good relationships.

4. An item to appear in the Parents' Newsletter to inform them of the campaign and request feedback from them.

5. Review the problem locations which the pupils have identified.

6. Approach the RE Department to identify aspects of their courses which support good relations.

7. Set up a fund to finance possible future INSET and publications.

8. Tutors to be trained specifically in approaches for countering bullying.

Comment

In both these schools the Educational Support Agencies can be seen acting in a pro-active way. From small beginnings came the development of a whole school approach in both schools. This whole school approach is important for it tells staff and pupils that they have an element of ownership of the procedures. One school found it necessary to develop a policy statement. Clearly, the school is used to working in that way. In the other school it was the strength and support of the pastoral system which gave the initiative its impetus. An important contributory factor in the development of these successful anti-bullying campaigns is the consultation with pupils. Without their commitment to making the campaigns successful, the initiatives would have been doomed.

3. Woodside Junior School, Waltham Forest

G. Riding, Headteacher
T. Alexander, Deputy Headteacher

Introduction

Although the impetus for the development of an anti-bullying programme came from within the school, unlike at the other two schools, the maintenance of the initiative was due to an LEA adviser who placed the initiative firmly within the community rather than the confines of the school.

The school is a co-educational primary school. The current role is 245 and rising. The buildings are almost 100 years old and all single-storey. The site is shared with an infant and nursery school and the two have a common Governing Body. Woodside serves a multicultural community, although a high percentage of the intake is from indigenous families who have lived in the area for generations.

3.1 The beginnings

A whole-school behaviour policy was planned as a response to an increase in the number of unpleasant playground incidents. It was a signal to parents and governors that the staff were not prepared to tolerate unacceptable behaviour. The intention was to involve parents and governors in the process and seek their support. The staff from the infant school were also interested in developing a behaviour policy, one which embodied the ideas set out in the Elton Report (1989), that is, a positive approach to the management of behaviour. INSET funds were released to pull the two institutions together with the aid of the Principal Educational Psychologist. The policy which was developed covered the following areas and issues for the junior school:

Movement around school
Being out of class
Consistency of approach
The Head's office
Playground
Praise and sanctions
Physical Education and swimming
Parental communications

Joint areas of concern were:

Dealing with kicking and verbal abuse
Playground issues
Health and Safety issues

The governors were consulted and the parents were informed of the school's intentions. The midday supervisors were also consulted prior to the document being published, to ensure a common policy for dealing with bullying and other forms of unacceptable behaviour, implemented by all adults in the school in a consistent way.

The school had also initiated Record of Achievement folders, which were well-received by staff and pupils alike. The RoAs encouraged children to comment on their progress and sought parental views. Even though the aims of the record had been explained to parents through the school's newsletter, the parents, for a variety of reasons, felt that this particular form of motivating their children was insufficient. The school needed something more tangible to present to governors, parents and children.

3.2 The LEA adviser

The aim was for the school to recognise the value of parents as the first educators of their children and to provide positive statements of what parents could expect of staff, via the RoAs or the school handbook. But in the attempt to pull together a behavioural policy, an anti-bullying programme, a Record of Achievement and improved home-school links, it was feared that the staff might lose sight of the original objectives. This was compounded by 'London Disease', namely, the rapid turnover of staff.

The Headteacher invited the LEA adviser to come into school for a 'focused visit' — not a full inspection. The adviser's brief was to give an overview of parental involvement and offer advice on how to improve it. Any negative attitude was noted by the adviser. Just as we need to encourage pupils to tell us about problems they are having with bullies, so we need parents to feel confident that the school will take their worries seriously if they do make a complaint and that the staff will act on it. The negative attitudes the adviser identified were:

> Attitudes of some teachers towards parents
>
> Increased socio/economic pressures, including the need for both parents to be at work.
>
> Increased numbers of single parents.
>
> A lack of confidence and security felt by children.
>
> Parents' own negative experiences of school.

For their part the parents outlined the factors often overlooked by schools as trivial, which they felt encouraged them to become more involved in the life of the school, including the Record of Achievement and the anti-bullying programme and things such as:

'Being made to feel welcome.'

'A cup of tea.'

'Being told what to do and not being left in the air.'

Parents also made some positive comments. The school's newsletter was appreciated, because it was 'regular, informed, clear and read by a lot of people.' They also clearly welcomed the formal parents' evening, when as many as 90% of parents attended — a remarkably high percentage, showing the community's interest in the education of the children. They asked, however, for more detail and if possible more time with their children's teachers. The children too felt that parents' evenings were important and many remembered the points that had been made by their teachers the previous term. Such feedback is surely as important as that provided by the Record of Achievement.

To improve upon the generally sound home-school relationships, the adviser made a number of recommendations, some applying specifically to Woodside, but many applicable to most schools encouraging parental involvement when implementing an initiative such as an anti-bullying programme.

It is important to show parents the benefits of their involvement in the school's affairs. Schools which are able to encourage parents to take an active interest in their children's education will improve the life chances of their children. This needs to be reinforced regularly. The most effective way of doing this is to demonstrate those benefits in concrete terms. To show that the school is serious about parental involvement it must be seen in every aspect of school life. Some of these strategies are:

- Put up large notices reading 'Woodside School welcomes you' in several languages so that it can be clearly seen.
- Build a window hatch into the office or at least making the area where parents enter into school as welcoming as possible.
- Use a newsletter and make it as accessible as possible, even to parents who have reading difficulties. Pick out the important items with headings on paragraphs. Use plain English. Print key phrases in English and community languages.
- Keep in touch with local community organisations by ensuring they are visited regularly.
- Offer a programme of activities which attracts as wide a section of parents as possible.

Classroom practice can also be enhanced by parental involvement, but it needs to be done consistently and by all staff. This could be facilitated by having an INSET day devoted to the sharing of good practice among the staff. Some ways of encouraging parental involvement in their children's learning are:

■ Ensuring that teachers meet parents informally when they arrive and leave.

■ Developing a consistent approach to children taking books and other equipment home, making it clear to parents and children that this is important by using the Record of Achievement folder.

■ Drawing up guidelines for involving parents in class, assemblies and visits, playing particular attention to the needs of parents who lack confidence or are bilingual.

■ Keeping a list of parents who participate in classrooms or help in other ways or even display their photographs in the corridor or classroom.

■ Value the parents' involvement by buying a small present at the end of the year or sending a card at birthdays or religious festivals. A special social event could be held to celebrate the involvement of everyone at the school.

By adopting these measures, confidence between home and school can be developed over a relatively short time. Such confidence is one of the most powerful antidotes to bullying. The parents of bullies can be brought into the school within a background of good relationships and trust. If this is achieved, the parents will be more ready to believe the staff and be less defensive about certain aspects of their children's behaviour.

3.3 Evaluation

It soon became clear that the school was trying to develop a home-school partnership. A number of different elements were coming together in the school at one time. It was difficult pulling those strands together into one uniform development, perhaps because the staff were too 'close' to the developments to see a way forward. In instances like these, the use of an adviser or advisory team can be of enormous benefit, as happened at Woodside. The parents are given access to their children's learning and progress, and to the school's wider policies towards learning, discipline and extra-curricular activities. What emerged from this particular development of a home-school partnership became an integral part of the school's ethos. How a school begins that process depends on individual need. In this school it emerged from a focus on bullying.

The monitoring of such a development is not an easy task. However, since the increased involvement of parents in the life of the school is now one of the aims of the school, this is one performance indicator that can be easily collected. Others could include the frequency of use of the Record of Achievement by the parents. The way forward in Woodside now depends on the staff acting upon the adviser's recommendations and building into the school development plan a yearly review of their work.

4. The Ulster Quaker Peace Education Project

Seamus Farrell
John Lampen

Introduction

An unusual but no less effective way of influencing the behaviour of pupils comes from this initiative in Londonderry — a day-conference entitled 'Bullying: what can we do about it?' There were displays of posters by children and adults as well as stories written by children. The stories ranged from instances of teasing and being 'sent to Coventry' to criminal activity. In discussions it was learned — if nothing else — that the children have all the knowledge and insight necessary to analyse the subject. What they need is help to stop it.

4.1 The beginnings

The Quaker Peace Education Project (QPEP) is based at the University of Ulster in Londonderry. It is an action-research project of the University's Centre for the Study of Conflict and develops methods of conflict resolution, prejudice reduction and education for mutual understanding, for use in schools. Each year it invites every primary school in the city to send two pupils to a day conference — but not their teachers. The day is run by the Project's staff and volunteers, helped on this occasion by two student drama teachers from Stranmills Training College in Belfast.

The conference started with two warm-up exercises, the second being a problem solving exercise which left the children in six random groups with nine girls and boys in each group. Two members of the QPEP team were assigned to each group. In each group there was also an invited pupil from a second or third year of a local secondary school. Since all the pupil delegates start secondary school in the near future, it was thought that the older boys and girls would be a valuable source of information. Each child was asked to remember a time when he or she had been upset by being bullied or teased or called names or hurt by someone. Everyone, including the adults, shared their stories in pairs and each pair made a drawing of one or both of the stories (see page 152).

4.2 Implementing the Drama

The group was then asked to decide together which of their pictures to dramatise. The original idea had been to bring each mini-drama to its crisis point, stop the action and then appeal to the audience, 'What should s/he do now?' A practice workshop with secondary pupils the week before had given a salutary insight. It was found that the dramas had not only awoken very sharp memories, but also the accompanying feeling of paralysis. Even adults with years of experience of working with children had nothing to suggest, while the pupils had said, 'That's it — there's nothing you can do!' Someone then asked, 'Let's look at what's happening and why.' Immediately the discussion became animated instead of depressed. Ideas and memories began flowing. For the day conference each group leader was briefed to let the drama develop to the moment of bullying and then break off for discussion. To help the discussion the following guidelines were produced:

- Why is this happening?
- What do we feel about it?

One Day I was just minding my own business when a boy came over and told me to give him a sweet. But I said no so he started to call me names and scrape me. Then I went home crying

- Did we laugh while we watched the drama? If so why?
- How does the victim feel?
- Are some people more likely to be victims than others? Why?
- Is there something the victim could do to stop it?
- Is there anyone there — or near — who could stop it? How could the victim get help?
- Are grown-ups of any help at stopping bullying? What do they do that helps — or makes matters worse?
- When is it worth getting grown-up help?
- If there is a group involved does it involve leader(s) and followers? Do the followers always enjoy taking part? Why do they join in?
- Is there anyone in the group who might say 'That's enough!'? If someone does, will it usually stop it?
- Are there boys *and* girls in the bullying group? Are they behaving in the same way?
- In general are there differences in the way boys and girls bully?
- If there is regular bullying in school, who should take action to stop it? The pupils? The staff? The headteacher? A united approach?
- Do you have any ideas about how a united approach might be developed?
- Is violence necessary to stop violence? Or does it only leave people looking at how to get their own back?
- Does this discussion give us any ideas for continuing the drama in a way which will stop the bullying?

In the discussion the children talked about bullies and why they act as they do, acknowledging that they may in turn be victims, currently or in the past. They talked about their joining in with bullying gangs and the mixture of emotions they felt — fear of being another victim and revulsion at what they did, but also admitting to satisfaction. They told the other delegates that there is nearly always someone in the group who could (and often does) stop the bullying just by saying, 'That's enough.' They analysed the difference between the bullying gang and what they saw as 'real friendship'. They suggested that bullies need friends as much as punishment — many said 'Much more!' They looked at the advantages and disadvantages of telling teachers or parents. Opinions varied since some had had positive experiences whilst others had experienced only disappointment. They worried about the lack of skill which teachers and parents sometimes displayed when they tried to intervene. The secondary pupils told the younger delegates what it was like to start secondary school and reassured them that the more alarming

153

myths were untrue. Some children were already following the national debate on the subject. One boy told of a school in England which he had learned about from television, where there was a box into which the pupils could anonymously put the names of bullies.

4.3 The denouement

After the discussion had developed, each group returned to its drama and worked out a strategy for the victim or his/her friends. The conference was held in two large rooms, each of which contained three groups, so each group performed its drama for the other two. At the crisis point they paused and asked the audience for its comments and ideas and then presented their solution in dramatic form. Here are two examples.

1. Two primary school girls went to buy chips. They were passing a disco. Some older boys and girls coming out of the disco tried to get them to smoke a cigarette. When the girls resisted they were called 'chicken', 'cowards' and so on and threatened with a beating.

After a general discussion the group presented its own solution. One of the disco group who didn't like what was happening went back into the disco and told a bouncer, but asked him to pretend that he had noticed the incident himself. The informant did not return to the scene.

2. A boy in the dinner queue took the last chocolate bar. The boy behind him snatched it off his tray. When the first boy complained and asked for it back the other threatened him.'

Again the solution was discussed with the audience. The first boy's solution was to appeal to the rest of the queue: 'Do you think that's fair?' They supported him and it was grudgingly given back to him.

The dinner break followed. It is worth relating that one of the children had to go home because he was feeling unwell. It became clear that his tummy pains were related to the subject of the day. An asthmatic, nervous and insecure child, he had revealed that he hated school, 'Because I am always being picked on... laughed at... called a cissy... fatty... daddy's boy...' He had been afraid of attending the conference since he thought that pupils from other schools would treat him the same.

When he realised these fears were unfounded, he relaxed, but he had found the discussions about bullying just too painful. Teachers also need to be aware, as these delegates were, that some pupils will find the unveiling of the truths very painful. Such children need a lot of support and help.

Opposite: **Quaker Peace Education Project**
Primary Schools Conference on Bullying compiling 'what we would like to say to teachers about bullying'. (Photo: John Lampen)

Above: **Quaker Education Project**
Primary Schools Conference.
Role-Playing a bullying incident
—'What happened in the toilet'.
(Photo: John Lampen)

The afternoon session began with a co-operative game. Each 'room' presented one of its three dramas to the whole conference but without the break for discussion. Then the adults spaced themselves around the walls, each with a placard. The seven placards read as follows:

Some reasons why I used to be a bully.

How I stopped being a victim of bullying.

What we would say to *grown ups* who bully us.

What we would say about bullying to *teachers*.

What we would say about bullying to *bullies*.

What we would say about bullying to *victims*.

What we would say about bullying to *prefects and older children*.

The children were free to go to the topic of their choice. The adults were briefed to give as little prompting as possible except to encourage minority views to be heard. The results of these discussions were the core of the day's work and so they are listed in full below (page 158/159). The comments have been reordered and occasionally clarified but they represent the children's views entirely. Since everyone in the group was encouraged to speak, consistency of response was not looked for. However, there is a remarkably high level of agreement, which suggests that children themselves can come up with solutions if encouraged to do so.

Each group read its list to the whole gathering, using a small public address system. There was no challenge to the suggestions or discussion about whether they were sensible or not. This was deliberate. Instead the whole conference applauded each separate statement. One of the organisers then addressed the conference to summarise.

Opposite: **Quaker Peace Project**
Primary Schools Conference on Bullying — Group Discussion
(Photo: John Lampen)

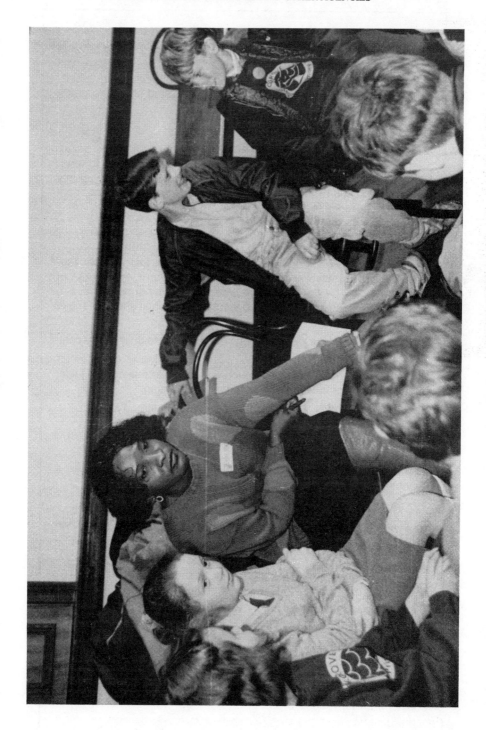

1. Some reasons why I used to be a bully

To get back on somebody; to get popular and attract girls and boys; to prove I was a winner; to get someone else into trouble; to smoke and encourage others; to have fun; to get attention and show off; to bully someone and blame it on them; because I wanted someone else's things; to get a group to batter someone; to act tough.

2. How I stopped being a victim

I ignored it; I stood up to them; I told my parents; I asked to learn self-defence; I phoned ChildLine; I got my friends to back me up; my big brother talked to the bullies; we had a class discussion; my best friends encouraged me.

3. What we would say to GROWN-UPS who bully us

JUST BECAUSE I AM A CHILD DOESN'T MEAN: I don't know anything; I have to slave about for parents when I'm in the middle of watching a film; I always have the time to go to the shops; I have to slave for the teachers; adults have the right to push in ahead of me in a queue.

Pick on someone your own size; why do you have to bully? Why can't you act your own age?

When the boys have a football match you tell us to make them juice; but when the girls have netball they make us nothing.

Because we are girls, it doesn't mean we can't do strong jobs.

I am really eleven — why won't you believe me?

4. What we would say about bullying to TEACHERS

Teachers should listen, not just punish.

The teachers should talk to the bully by him/herself.

Usually teachers get it wrong and punish the wrong person if they see something happening. (Sometimes they get it right; for example, children being bullied into smoking at one school got the issue discussed).

Have a box where we could put a note with the bullies' names.

Please give us a better hearing if we are bullied. Don't just say 'Stop telling tales' or 'It always happens.'

Get the whole class to tackle the subject (like we have today). Bring up the subject but don't mention names.

Teachers should set an example and not bully children themselves. Don't suspend bullies as they may be glad to get off school.

5. What we would say about bullying to BULLIES

A bully is really a coward.

Bullies bully for the fun, enjoyment, power and to make themselves feel cool.

Bullies have *no right* to have fun at other people's expense.

Bullying is not the way to get true friends. Bullying only gets you a bad reputation. Bullies don't get anything out of it and everybody else suffers.

Why not give up bullying and live a normal life?

6. What we would say about bullying to VICTIMS

Ignore them; agree with their remarks sarcastically; stay with a group of friends and get support from them; say 'What you say is what you are' or 'It takes one to know one'; avoid the bully; take up judo lessons or weight-lifting; forgive and forget; find out if the bully is jealous of you in some way; tell the bully to pick on someone his(her) own age and size; tell the bully you will not tell on him(her) if he(she) stops; report it to an adult.

7. What we would say about bullying to PREFECTS AND OLDER CHILDREN

Please protect us against bullying; tell the teachers about bullying; make teachers aware who the bullies are.

Stop younger children bullying even younger ones; make bullies wear badges saying: 'I'm a bully — keep away'; make them feel small; stop bullies enjoying themselves; take bullies' friends away; make them see that other people are doing nice things and being rewarded for them; punish them only if it's going to help. Prefects should report them.

Reassure the victim — it won't go on forever.

Talk to the victim about the bully and his(her) problems. Maybe he(she) is the one with the biggest problem and the two of them could become friends.

No-one could expect a one day conference to solve the problem of bullying. However, all the delegates had shared a huge amount of experience and understanding and many positive ideas emerged from the day, which the organisers hoped the delegates would try. Two children reported: 'We were glad to be chosen to attend but we did not really know what to expect. We thought it might be boring. We felt nervous before leaving school but once there we were OK. The day went better than we expected and we enjoyed it... We found out that there are different kinds of bullying and that we were at times bullies ourselves. It made us feel sorry for anyone who is bullied because nobody likes being picked on. Also we realised it is hard for people to tell anyone if they are being bullied.'

Another pupil, with her teacher's help, wrote a letter to the LEA asking them to take stronger action to prevent bullying. What an LEA can do to help prevent bullying is explored elsewhere in this book.

Comment

The Quaker Peace Education Project is committed to a whole-school approach to bullying. The evidence from this conference shows that pupils can play an active part in this. Bullying puts many children (not only the victims, but the spectators and some of the bullies) under such pressure that they would be grateful for the introduction of a policy in which they have a positive role to play. Children have a great deal to contribute, if safe and imaginative ways can be found for them to share their insights into bullying. Although few schools are lucky enough to have such a project on their doorstep to guide their attempts at countering bullying, the ideas presented here can be incorporated by means of drama lessons or an imaginative PSE programme. That the children themselves can come up with effective ways of countering bullying should come as no surprise. What teachers and other adults have to do is listen to children.

Theme Five

Local Education Authorities

Introduction

In the *Guardian* of May 20,1992, Michael Marland wrote:

> Last month some newspapers reported that the Department of Education had 'launched a campaign'. All that had happened was that Eric Forth, schools minister, expressed some platitudes and welcomed an 'anti-bullying' pack put out with Gulbenkian–British Telecom backing.
>
> But Mr. Forth ought to have been ashamed that it was left to others. The Government has been slow to act on bullying in the same, practical way as other European governments which can demonstrate sharp reductions in its incidence.

Just as the government has failed to act on bullying in our schools, so have some Local Education Authorities been sadly remiss in adopting pro-active approaches to the problem. Schools can share common experiences and will look to the LEA to provide a lead or perhaps monitor the process in schools across the authority. The following research notes two different, but thoughtful and thought-provoking, LEA responses, one in a mainly rural area, the other in a large city.

161

In Gwynedd the pro-active approach adopted facilitated individual schools to address their particular problems. The approach allowed for experimentation and trialling and for effective practice to be disseminated. Thus the authority provided strategic planning for schools in Gwynedd and was able to offer advice in: management strategies for dealing with bullying; curricular approaches for dealing with bullying, including classroom strategies, pupil grouping, and materials; and problems associated with transition. Furthermore, the Authority's support services became an avenue for dealing with bullying.

Lothian was the first authority in Britain to tackle bullying in schools in a concerted way. Local business, the Lothian Police Department and the Education Authority combined their resources to produce the 'Travelling Roadshow', a video and teaching resource pack. This has proved so successful that it requires an agent to handle the delivery of the work. Lothian has also registered another impressive first: following on with the first Children's Charter in the UK, when the production and monitoring of separate charters has a high political priority.

1. Gwynedd Education Authority
Anwen Lloyd, Education Officer

Since the 1988 Education Reform Act, schools have been overwhelmed by the time-consuming and culture-changing requirements of Local Management of Schools and the introduction of the National Curriculum. At the same time, local education authorities have been engaged in preparing schools to become autonomous establishments and have evolved a more monitorial role. In this context of rapid and fundamental change it would have been easy to postpone attention to such matters as classroom and behaviour management.

Not so, Gwynedd. Its general education aims may be summarised as follows:

> The provision of education of the highest possible quality for all Gwynedd pupils in accordance with their age, ability, interest and aptitude, so that they become rounded personalities, develop and use all their talents and equip themselves to be responsible members of a bilingual community.

The Authority clearly sees its role as the facilitator and disseminator of good practice. It has enabled schools to consider areas they wish to develop and to trial various strategies under the wider umbrella of the Education Committee's stated policy and guidelines.

The statutory abolition of corporal punishment provided an opportunity for the Education Authority to examine its attitude towards discipline in schools and a working party identified the roles of schools, governors and the Authority. The report of the working party in 1988 promoted discussion within the Authority's schools and governor training sessions. The report sought to define the role of the school and governing body in maintaining discipline and order on the one hand, and of the Education Authority on the other, in supporting the school by co-ordinating the contribution of the support agencies.

In *Education Observed 5* (DES,1987) Her Majesty's Inspectorates note that:

> The ethos or climate of a school is central to the establishment and maintenance of high standards of behaviour.

The ethos of a school is based on the quality of the relationships between the teachers themselves and between teachers and pupils. The report identifies three key elements to a positive ethos :

■ the example set by teachers and other adults
■ teachers' expectations

■ the leadership of the Headteacher.

Their effects are prominent in the life of the school in many ways, for example:

■ the aims and policies of the school
■ the positive support given to pupils
■ the school's pastoral care provision
■ the assistance given to teachers
■ the school's environment and resources.

HMI related the quality of the curriculum to pupil's behaviour. A broad curriculum with varied activities suited to the needs of each pupil and enthusiastically presented, can be a challenge demanding constant attention and leaving no time for misbehaviour or an interest in bullying.

The Authority's working party considered the following factors to be essential to the promotion of good behaviour in our schools:

■ Factors involving the curriculum, such as quality, relevance, the grouping of pupils, the selection of teachers, teaching methods, record keeping, assessment and the skill of individual teachers.

■ The pastoral system which aims at supporting pupils rather than reacting to crises.

■ The general ethos of the establishment, as promoted through the leadership of the Headteacher and senior staff; the relationship between pupils and staff; an environment of high standards of behaviour, emphasising rewards not sanctions. Amongst the many recommendations was that the school should regularly review its policy in relation to discipline. The confidence of the parents and the community, as well as the agreed support of each member of staff in implementation, is essential for success. Each governing body should ensure that expertise in disciplinary matters is developed by at least a proportion of its members, who can then give prompt assistance to the Headteacher when required.

1.1 The beginnings

The working party's exploration of discipline and order in schools was followed by the Elton Report with strikingly similar recommendations. Together, these reports provided a vehicle for work in the field of behaviour management, and support for pupils became one of the Authority's priorities in its development plan. The list of priorities was agreed between the Authority, the schools and their governors, thereby ensuring a common ownership of the objectives. An Education Support Grant from the Welsh

Office was not forthcoming but the In-Service Training Grant and the Local Development Fund generated much good work on classroom management and behaviour problems in and around the school premises— hence the emphasis on bullying.

Bullying had already received attention in Gwynedd since public awareness of the harmful effects of bullying was mirrored by professional concern amongst teachers and support staff attached to the Authority. In 1989 the Health Authority's Child and Family Guidance Service was invited to run an in-service course for the Education Psychology Service and the Educational Welfare Service. An overwhelming case for further action was highlighted by the results of research in South Yorkshire and Strathclyde, where estimates of the numbers of children suffering at the hands of bullies were appallingly high. Awareness of the effects of bullying on individuals over a number of years had also increased, together with the realisation that bullies are more likely to commit serious crimes than their peers. Finally, evidence gathered by Olweus in Norway, that effective action can dramatically reduce the incidence of bullying, led to the establishing of an advisory group chaired by the Chief Educational Psychologist and including a primary school headteacher, secondary school deputy headteacher, primary adviser, an education officer, education welfare officers, a psychiatrist from the Child and Family Guidance Service and a representative from the Psychology Department of the University College of North Wales. Advisory contributions were received from a North Wales Police Inspector and one of the editors(DT).

This enthusiastic and cohesive group embarked on several initiatives, including:

- a questionnaire for schools
- a booklet: 'Tackling Bullying in Schools'
- a pamphlet for parents
- a policy guide for schools
- a personal and social education module
- advising a theatre in education group.

A lecturer in the Psychology Department of University College of North Wales was commissioned to devise a bilingual questionnaire for research purposes and to help individual schools identify and reduce the level of bullying (see page 166-168). The questionnaire can be used at any time by Gwynedd schools, once the research sample has been completed, so it is a valuable long-term resource, which can target specific year groups across the Authority.

BULLYING

BULLYING IS ANY ACT WHICH IS INTENDED TO HURT, THREATEN OR FRIGHTEN SOMEONE ELSE.

The survey that follows is about 'bullying' in schools. Many children are bullied by others in ways that can make them very unhappy, and the survey is intended to find out how much bullying takes place in schools in Gwynedd and what sorts of things bullies do to other children. That information will help us to decide how we can try to reduce the amount of bullying that goes on.

We would like you to answer the questions below as accurately as you can. **We don't want your name and we have no way of finding out your identity, so you can be completely honest.**

If anything like this has happened to you please tell us about it by answering the questions below. Everything will be treated as completely confidential.

1. Have you ever been bullied at school or on your way to and from school?

   1☐ Yes, very often 2☐ Yes, often 3☐ Yes, sometimes 4☐ Yes, only a little
   5☐ No **(If 'no' go straight to question 13)**

2. If 'yes' have you been bullied (Tick only one box)

   1☐ More than once, by the same bullies?
   2☐ More than once, by different bullies?

3. Which things have bullies done to you? (Tick as many boxes as you need)

   1☐ a deliberate push 1☐ punching 1☐ kicking
   1☐ insulting or 'calling names' 1☐ hiding or stealing things you own
   1☐ deliberately ignoring you 1☐ making fun of you
   1☐ threatening to hurt you 1☐ staring at you
   1☐ something else (give as many details as you can) ....

   ....

4. At what age were you bullied? (Tick as many as you need)

   1☐ under five 1☐ 5 - 8 years 1☐ 9- 12 years 1☐ over 12 years

5. What age were the bullies? (Tick as many as you need)

   1☐ same age as you 1☐ older then you 1☐ younger than you

6. Were they boys or girls? (Tick as many as needed)

   1☐ boys only 1☐ girls only 1☐ both boys and girls

7. When was the last time you were bullied? (Tick only one box)

    1☐ today   2☐ in the last week or two   3☐ 2 - 4 weeks ago
    4☐ more than a month ago   5☐ More than 6 months ago

8. In what places have you been bullied? (Tick as many boxes as you need to)

    1☐ going to or from school   1☐ in the school playground   1☐ at lunch
    1☐ in the toilets   1☐ in the classroom
    1☐ other (please give details) ....

9. How much bother has bullying caused you? (Tick only one box)

    1☐ no problem   2☐ it made you a little worried   3☐ it made you very worried
    4☐ it was so bad you didn't want to go to school

10. Did you ever tell anybody that you were being bullied? (Tick as many as you need)

    1☐ parent   1☐ teacher   1☐ head teacher   1☐ doctor
    1☐ friends   1☐ never told anyone

(If you ticked 'never told anyone' go straight to question 12)

11. Did telling anyone lead to the bullying being stopped

    1☐ Yes   2☐ No

(Now go straight to question 13)

12. If you didn't tell anyone was that because....... (tick as many as you need to)

    1☐ you were afraid of the bullies   1☐ you thought you could deal with it yourself
    1☐ you thought nobody would listen   1☐ there was some other reason

13. What do you think of children who bully others?

    1☐ feel sorry for them   2☐ dislike them
    3☐ no feeling for them   4☐ admire them

14. Who is <u>most</u> responsible for stopping bullying from happening?

    1☐ the bully   2☐ the bully's parents   3☐ the teachers
    4☐ the headteacher   5☐ the victim   6☐ children other than the bully or victim who are in the same class

15. Are you   1☐ a boy   or   2☐ a girl?

16. How old are you?   ☐ 11   ☐ 12   ☐ 13   ☐ 14   ☐ 15
    ☐ 16

17. Approximately how tall are you?

    [＿＿＿] cm or ☐ ft ☐ ins

18. Approximately how much do you weigh?

    [＿＿＿] kilos or [＿＿＿] lbs

19. Have you ever bullied anyone?

    1☐ Yes, often   2☐ Yes, sometimes   3☐ Yes, once or twice
    4☐ No, never

20. What, if anything, should be done about stopping bullying?

    ....
    ....
    ....
    ....
    ....

Gwynedd's schools are bilingual so guidelines in Welsh were needed. This would help to encourage a sense of ownership. The Deputy Head in the working party compiled the Welsh guidelines —since published in convenient booklet form — after consultation with schools and elected members, adapting passages from *Bullying: A Positive Response* with the authors' permission. The Guidelines identify the characteristics of bullies, describe relevant research, suggest strategies to help prevent bullying, provide a self-protection checklist for victims and suggest actions for teachers to take in response to bullying incidents.

It was felt that parents were often reluctant to report bullying for fear of reprisals against their children so would give children misguided advice. A pamphlet has been produced for schools to distribute to parents and for Educational Psychologists and Educational Welfare Officers to use. It aims to reassure parents that bullying is taken seriously and will not be tolerated by schools and provides information on how to seek assistance for dealing with incidents of bullying.

Showing its commitment to the reduction of bullying, the Education Committee approved the Policy Guide for School. This gives the Authority's standpoint on bullying and suggestions on how schools might formulate whole-school policies for the attention of pupils, parents, staff and governors. The level of participation in the debate by the elected members certainly showed that bullying is regarded as very serious and a highly charged subject.

A Personal and Social Education module was devised for use by pupils in the Year 7. Four main themes emerged:

Friendship — making and keeping friends
Disagreement
Gang leaders
Fear

Various teaching methods are suggested, including role-play, discussion, drama within tutorial periods or during language or art lessons. The module concludes with case studies that provide an opportunity to assess the pupils' comprehension of the subtler aspects, such as taking responsibility, compromising, leadership skills and assertiveness.

Gwynedd support Cwmni'r Frân Wen, a theatre in education (TIE) company which tours schools with three different productions annually. For its production on assertiveness within the context of bullying and abuse, the Education Authority seconded a teacher to create a classroom pack to accompany the TIE primary school play. Teachers were prepared beforehand in a series of workshops. It became apparent that the play was viewed with some trepidation since some of the scenes were quite powerful. The feed-back, however, showed that it had been an immense success.

The advisory group feels that it has achieved its aims and acted as a catalyst for schools. The resources in terms of guidelines and teaching aids are available for use in every school in Gwynedd. Hopefully, behavioural management and bullying will appear in school development plans as features that require constant reviewing along with the statutory require-ments concerning the implementation of the National Curriculum.

1.2 Practical Implementation in Schools

The Education Authority invited applications for the funding of projects on 'Managing Pupils' Behaviour' which would meet the recommendations made in the Authority's report on Discipline and Order in Schools and in the Elton Report. Ten schools were selected to run pilot schemes under the management of the Secondary Sector's Development Group. They con-tracted to provide: information as required for monitoring purposes by the Authority; a detailed report for dissemination by the authority; the formula-tion or revision of the school's policy for consideration by the governing body; and to participate in further in-service training. It was agreed that the authority would own the copyright of any publications resulting from the scheme. The schools produced examples of a complete overhaul of pastoral care practices; the need to monitor and develop classroom practice; the re-evaluation of the pupils' role, participation and sense of ownership of the school, including assemblies, libraries, breaktimes, movement around school and the curriculum. Apart from the obvious implications for general discipline the issue of bullying was also specifically addressed:

- Parents of Year 7 pupils were interviewed and a contract negotiated between school, parents and pupil, thus alerting parents to their responsibility for their child's behaviour and attitude, while alerting pupils to the need for them to respect one another at all times. This exercise led to discussions with the primary feeder schools about a common approach to expectations of pupil behaviour.
- A two-day staff conference followed by the formulation of a working party to review school policy. Topics discussed included: differential teaching, preventative approaches, gender issues, integration of pu-pils with special educational needs and classroom management.
- Co-operation with a feeder primary school to identify some of the characteristics of the transfer group in order to monitor behaviour and take pro-active steps to discourage negative interaction.
- An investigation into the reasons for under-achievement, truancy and absconding. This was followed by the devising of various strategies

for dealing with the underlying causes, the commonest of which was bullying.

■ A home-school strategy to complement the work of the Educational Welfare Officer. For example, a problem relating to the discipline would warrant a home visit by a member of staff to parents who viewed school with suspicion.

■ Producing a questionnaire on bullying for pupils in Years 7, 8 and 9 with an invited assessor. The questionnaire was completed anonymously but the child's gender and tutor group were indicated. The 95% response gave the school insights into the scale of the problem. The pupils were asked to suggest methods of dealing with the bullies. Their suggestions, in order of preference were:

Year 7: telling a teacher
         detention
         community tag
         self-defence lessons

Year 8: telling a teacher
         detention
         anti-bullying squad
         attention of the child psychologist/
         psychiatrist

Year 9: helping the bullies
         exclusion from school
         detention
         bully court
         torture!

It was discovered that most instances of bullying occurred in the school yard during breaktimes, and a few on the bus to and from school. Girls complained mostly about name-calling, boys mostly about physical bullying, mainly kicks in the groin. This echoes larger-scale research across the country. Sixty pupils were named as bullies by their peers. All pupils who took part were offered counselling by the assessor. Of the 21 pupils who accepted, some had been identified as bullies by their peers. The pupils were then advised to discuss their concerns with their Head of Year or Form Tutor.

This exercise culminated in a conference for governors, parents, staff, senior pupils, primary sector representatives and an education officer. A policy on bullying was planned and the school's anti-bullying resources for tutorial lessons were exhibited.

■ Generating a catchment area policy on bullying to ensure consistency of approach and to display resolve to combat bullying. This project was enthusiastically carried out by a cross-section of senior school management, who saw bullying as a discrete problem in the area.

1.3 Evaluations

In order to disseminate good practice, discuss projects which did not come up to expectations and generally raise awareness across the county, two conferences were arranged.

The first was designed to allow schools to discuss their experiences and was therefore very much an 'in-house' conference. Representatives of secondary schools which had taken part in the pilot scheme gave accounts of their work and there were brief talks on general discipline and ethos, bullying and the support services. Workshops looked at policy, staff development, school organisation and links with agencies and support services. Evaluations were positive and enthusiastic, although some people had been wary of in-service training in this field. It was clear after the two days that classroom and behaviour management training would be given higher priority in future.

The second, shorter, conference was for a representative sample of the primary sector. Referrals from the primary sector had significantly increased across the Authority, indicating that behavioural problems and bullying had become a problem for Headteachers. Another working party was set up to consider strategies to overcome the problem.

Managing pupil behaviour is now a constant issue in the Authority and bullying is clearly part of it. The Authority provides support by means of:

the Educational Psychological Service
the Education Welfare Service
the Schools Section through its responsibility for pupils, parents and the helpline system
the governor training programme
prioritisation in the Authority's Annual Programme
in-service training.

Gwynedd Education Authority in its role as facilitator and strategic planner, has usefully prevented the duplication of projects and provided support and encouragement. Initiatives are managed by the relevant sector Development Group, which includes representative Headteacher, officers and advisers. This raises the status of work on bullying. Much is in the hands of individual schools, but through its monitoring function, the Authority can ask questions and prompt an ethos in all the schools that will allow pupils to learn without hindrance or distress.

2. Lothian Regional Council

Carolyn Bennett, Headteacher

Introduction

Lothian Regional Council has shown itself to be a very innovative authority regarding protection of children. It was the first local authority in Scotland to address the problem of bullying and as early as 1989 produced an anti-bullying resource pack called SPEAK-UP. More recently, it has pioneered the first Children's Family Charter in the UK, concerned with wide-ranging children's rights, including the right to be able to attend school and not be subjected to abuse and humiliation.

SPEAK-UP: An anti-bullying resource pack

2.1 The beginnings

Following successful Crime Prevention Panel Meetings in South Edinburgh, a local Councillor and the Headteacher of a local primary school decided to try to involve primary school children in caring about crime in their community. With the help of a confidential questionnaire, P7 pupils (10-11 years) were asked what they feared most in their own community. The list was long and revealing. However, glue sniffing, theft, vandalism, fear of gangs and bullying were universal, with bullying top of the list. It became obvious that children of all ages needed to be given strategies to help them cope with their fear of bullying and with pressure from their own peers to get into trouble.

In 1989 an active partnership was formed between members of the South Edinburgh Crime Prevention Panel, a Regional Councillor, the Community Police, private business sector, voluntary agencies, staff, parents and pupils of a Lothian Region High School and its feeder Primary schools, in order to raise the consciousness of children and young adults about bullying in their local area and in their schools.

Young children learn quickly from role-play and dramatisation of events, so it was decided that P7 and S1 pupils from Liberton High School and its associated cluster primary schools — Fernieside, Gilmerton, Liberton and Moredun — should together produce an original musical drama which would tour the area, showing children how to confront the problems of bullying.

2.2 Development

The Travelling Roadshow was an original musical drama on bullying, professionally directed. Staff in the schools were far too busy to direct a project of this scale. The Roadshow had to be imaginative, modern and colourful, capturing the imagination. A freelance drama worker, with experi-

ence in youth and community theatre, was invited to write and direct the Roadshow, lyrics and music, with the assistant headteacher of one of the primary schools who also acted as Musical Director.

The Roadshow toured schools in south Edinburgh, encouraging children to confront problems of bullying and particularly to speak up and seek help from adults. The musical drama, called *It's No Just Rough and Tumble* has a clear, straightforward message. Kelly is a normal, outgoing primary school kid until she falls foul of 'Rotten Ross' McBride and his gang of bullies. Threatened and frightened, she lies to her parents and coerces her own sister into silence. Help is at hand when troubled sleep gives way to a fantasy Warrior of Rap who provides her with a good self-defence, and the confidence to say 'NO'!

Songs, dance, drama and fun combine to get the message across — to the victimised *and* the culprits — that school bullying is an abuse which must not be kept a secret. Bullies and their victims both need help; left alone, bullying leads directly to many problems in adulthood.

The Travelling Roadshow served many purposes. Pupils from different schools met and made friends. The involvement of the Police Department showed the audience that the Police are approachable and are there to support and protect. The community benefitted as people worked together to improve the quality of their own lives. The songs, dance and mime had their own value but most of all, the Travelling Roadshow enabled performers and audience to grow in confidence and self-esteem. In addition, it encouraged the children to feel that they, as well as adults, have rights and should be able to say 'NO' to bullies.

The initiative was sponsored by local private businesses, the Crime Prevention Panel, the Safer Edinburgh Campaign and by Lothian Region Education Department. The Community Police transported the cast to and from rehearsals and performances.

Because of the enormous interest in the Roadshow and in order to spur on other communities to tackle the problem of bullying, a resource pack was produced for schools and agencies caring for children. The pack includes a documentary video of the roadshow, the video transcript, a cassette of the musical score, the play script, the musical score, ideas for drama for P1-S2 pupils (5-14 years), teacher/youth leader notes for P1-S2, worksheets for P1-S2, and research and background reading on bullying eg. *Bullying — A Positive Response*. The pack also includes a SPEAK-UP poster, pen and stickers promoting the SPEAK-UP message.

The launch of the pack was widely publicised in local and national newspapers, Police and Community and Regional Council newsletters and magazines, and on radio and nation-wide television.

The pack is now on its third print run and has sold to schools, Crime Prevention Panels, Child Psychologists, Community and Social workers, Community Police Departments, School Boards, PTA's and to individual parents throughout Great Britain and Ireland.

2.3 Evaluation

Schools in the Edinburgh area using the pack report definite changes in attitudes towards bullying. Teaching and ancillary staff know how to handle complaints and pupils know that their problems will be taken seriously. Staff also report that the pupils have gained in confidence and their sense of self-esteem has improved.

The success of the pack has, however, caused huge administrative problems for the original organising team. When it became obvious that demand for the pack would continue for some time, the team approached Dundee-based SCCC, which reached many agencies caring for children, to find out if it would take over production of the pack. (For details see page 177.)

Children's Family Charter

In June 1992 the Lothian Children's Family Charter was launched by Lothian Regional Council and Lothian Health Authority. Young people in Lothian now have direct access to an independent adjudicator if they feel they are mistreated by peers or adults — including teachers, social workers or health professionals. The Charter sets out exactly what children under 16 years can expect from those services.

The 24-page document is based on the 1989 United Nations Convention on the Rights of the Child and covers everything from the right to play safely to the right to an education free from abuse and harassment. School pupils were consulted and invited to define the rights they wanted and to frame them in ways that could be easily understood.

Some responses were blunt:

> *All children have a right to attend a good school which is colourful and interesting, with teachers who care about all children.*

Others were practical:

> *Children should be allowed some say about what happens in school — reports, library, books, bullies, foreign languages and school dinners.*

Some replies were profound and deeply perceptive:

> *Every child has a right to a loving and caring family, which protects them from harm, but encourages children to grow up to be independent people.*

Nobody should take advantage of the fact that you are a child.

No-one has the right to take your hopes away.

The principles behind the Charter have been supported by 40 organisations, including Save the Children, Barnardo's, the Scottish Child and Family Alliance, and the Churches. Among the rights suggested under the Charter are the right to:

1. Appeal against all decisions regarding their welfare to an independent adjudicator.
2. Give or withhold consent to their own adoption if aged 12 or over.
3. Avoid punishment which diminishes their dignity; pupils should not be made to feel foolish or write repetitive lines.
4. Freedom from racial, sexual and religious harassment.
5. Access to information held on record concerning them.
6. Reasonable waiting times at hospitals, limited to 30 minutes as an out-patient.

These are far-reaching rights which challenge the preconceptions and attitudes of parents, teachers, nurses, social and welfare workers. For as the region's education convenor and one of the Charter's principle architects observes:

> These are real entitlements to empower children, to encourage them to explore their rights and to provide a code of conduct which helps give them a sense of their own individual worth. It will take many years to change attitudes fundamentally, but this is a start in that process.

Editorial Comment

We have charters for parents, patients and other adults but what rights do our children have? Before bullying can be stopped in schools, the attitudes of adults towards aggression, the bullies, and the victims, must be challenged. This local initiative can be commended to other authorities in the UK and to government departments.

(SPEAK-UP is available from the Scottish Consultative Council on the Curriculum, Gardyne Road, Dundee, DD5 1NY.)

Reflections and Perceptions

Graham Herbert

The approaches outlined have been wide-ranging, creative and thoughtful. They sought to tackle problems of bullying as it affected pupils in individual schools, in clusters of schools or across Local Education Authorities. The editors' categorisation into separate themes and approaches is in some ways misleading. Minsthorpe High School could as easily have been placed in the management theme rather than transition; equally, the work by the Quaker Peace Education Project could fit the curriculum theme as easily as the one on the use of outside agencies. The initiatives outlined throughout this book can, however, be distilled into a similar format, although the emphasis in each one is slightly different, depending on historical, organisational and environmental circumstances.

1. Raising awareness

In every initiative the first task has been to raise the awareness of all the people involved. It has been done in a variety of ways. Some schools initially purchased materials for individual staff — a particularly successful strategy in small schools like Shirehampton and raising awareness very cost effectively in schools with tight budgets. Larger schools opted to provide in-service courses for staff. These models too, have varied. Some schools held full school INSET days, to include Governors and other adults in regular contact with pupils, such as lunchtime supervisors. Other schools have combined in-service training with hand-outs of summaries of relevant materials. Other schools used questionnaires, to provide staff with hard evidence of the extent and nature of bullying in their school. This book has numerous examples, all concerned to elicit open and truthful responses. Whatever the approach, raising the awareness and challenging assumptions of staff about the extent and nature of bullying is crucial. It is not just physical attacks that pupils construe as bullying, but also name-calling, sleights to family, deliberate attempts to frighten and so on. Above all, it is any form of behaviour which, in La Fontaine's (1991) words, 'conveys a message: one of rejection and hostility ...The bullied child then feels isolated and lonely'.

The following anecdote will seem familiar and highlights the complex nature of bullying behaviour. Alice and her best friend, Rachael, do everything together. They sit together during registration. They always work together. They spend their spare time together. They stay at each other's house at the weekends. They even go on holiday together. Because of the girls' friendship, their parents are also friendly. One weekend, unbeknown to their parents, the girls had a slight argument and parted without making up. Next Monday at school, Alice and Rachael are not speaking. Rachael has gathered a group of girls in the same class and is divulging some of Alice's best kept secrets, like what she really thought about Sandra's new hairstyle! During registration Alice and Rachael sit in their accustomed places and everything appears normal to their teacher.

But no-one is talking to Alice. At first she just ignores it and carries on as usual. She works diligently, as all the pupils do. Rachael and the other girls are their usual lively selves, swapping tales and telling secrets but no-one is talking to Alice. By break, Alice is becoming frustrated and angry. Whenever she speaks — asking for a felt tip, a rubber, a pencil sharpener — no-one responds. The other girls sense they are having an impact upon Alice and so they follow her at break. She shouts at them in anger and frustration: 'Go away! Leave me alone!'

Sandra asks, 'Did someone speak?'

Rachael replies: 'I never heard anything. It must have been the wind.'

After break the girls are in their usual positions, working industriously. Again, everything seems normal, except that no-one is talking to Alice. One sensitive teacher notices that Alice is not her usual self and asks if anything is amiss. Alice can hardly say: 'No-one is speaking to me!' So she just shrugs, says; 'I don't feel very well,' and carries on with her work. This kind of treatment continues throughout the day. She suffers six and a half hours of isolation, rejection and misery, much of it under the noses of the staff and many do not even notice. At the end of school, Alice runs home and sobs on her mother's shoulder: 'I'm never going back there again.'

All of us must come to accept that a series of incidents like this constitutes bullying of the worst order. Alice was never hit or kicked or punched, No threats were made. But everyone can associate with Alice's misery, isolation and rejection. Bullying is indeed a complex behaviour, dependent upon complex social interactions. There may be other occasions when Alice and Rachael do not talk for an entire day, during an examination period for example, but the lack of chatter between Alice and Rachael will not end in Alice's despair. All adults in school need to become sensitive to the social interactions of pupils, to prevent Alice and children like her from being isolated. We must give such pupils the confidence to complain or admit that something is going wrong. We must also give the other pupils, like the ones who took Rachael's side, the confidence to say, 'We don't do that here.'

2. Indicators of success

The schools in this report identified the indicators that their programme of combating bullying was having effect in the school. These success criteria took many forms. In some cases it proved difficult to devise specific criteria, particularly when looking at effects of the work in the general community. However, certain indicators some of the schools looked for *can* be transferred to other institutions. For example, Eastbourne School took as one of its performance indicators that the school be a 'Telling School'. They looked for an *increase* in the number of referrals since, if they were generating a 'telling' ethos, then pupils were evidently encouraged to report any incidences of bullying.

A further measure of success is how pupils engage with the curriculum materials about bullying. The materials developed by St John Wall RC Comprehensive, which have become part of their PSE, act as one such indicator. That pupils wrote their feelings about this work in their Records of Achievement is testimony to the positive approach such work generates. Woodside Junior School looked to the greater involvement of the parents as one measure of its success. This is potentially a problematic and value-laden criterion. However, if the involvement of parents is to include such things as their increasing use of Records of Achievement and not only attendance at fund-raising functions, then such criteria can be easily measured and monitored. At Glapton School an anecdote about improved patterns of behaviour in the community served to reflect the success of the programme being implemented.

The advantage of determining the success criteria *before* the programmes are implemented is twofold. In the first instance the success criteria reinforce the argument that an anti-bullying campaign will have positive effects upon pupils' behaviour. As we saw at Minsthorpe, some staff remain sceptical about the need for, or efficacy of, a programme to counter bullying. The editors take the view that, 'it is a basic entitlement of all children and young people in the United Kingdom that they receive their education free from humiliation, oppression and abuse' (Tattum & Herbert, 1990). Nevertheless, we cannot expect that everyone takes on board these values. For those who do not, success criteria can be a reflection of positive achievements. In the second instance, the choice of effective success criteria helps reinforce the team's efforts to implement them by acting as short-term goals and maintaining momentum.

3. Implementation

Implementation of these programmes has followed a similar pattern. After raising the staff's and pupils' awareness and pointing out the benefits the school can hope to realise, the next task is to implement the policy in a way which gives everyone in the school some form of ownership of the process. There will be short, medium and long term developments.

Short term developments have usually begun with some form of audit, such as use of a questionnaire. Such strategies can serve two functions — helping identify the situation in school, and showing staff and pupils the nature of the problem as it affects their lives. This was done effectively at Malvern Girls' College. This needs to be followed with some kind of system being developed that suits the needs of the individual school — as shown in the model (page 183).

A variety of methods can work. Some schools have opted for written records, others for the 'post box' device. Whichever system is adopted, it needs to satisfy these criteria:

- ■ Who will intervene and how?
- ■ What form of recording will be used?
- ■ Where will this be completed and where will it be stored?
- ■ When will the records be made?
- ■ How will the adults act towards the protagonists?
- ■ Why is the process seen as important by the school?

An effective system will also provide valuable information to the school about:

- ■ Who is involved in the bullying
- ■ When bullying is taking place
- ■ Where bullying is taking place
- ■ What forms the behaviour takes

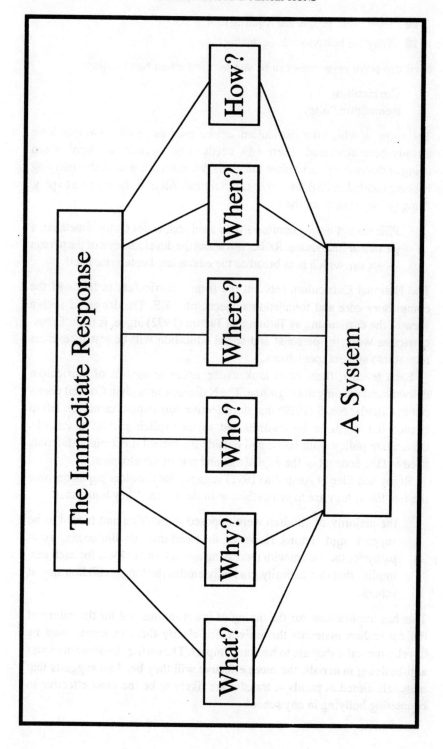

■ How other people are reacting to it
■ Why the behaviour is occurring.

Medium term responses can be summarised under two headings:

Curriculum
Behaviour Policy

The ways in which the curriculum can be used as an effective tool have already been described. There now needs to be a cautionary word, when using or developing curriculum materials. We must not assume that bullying is being tackled in PSE lessons or tutorial time. All of us have a role to play. Pring (1988) points out that:

> PSE should not be confused with a subject, a slot on the timetable, a particular innovation. Rather is it about the developments of the person — an aim which is as broad as the educational enterprise itself.

The National Curriculum sets out the formal curriculum in terms of the compulsory core and foundation subjects, plus RE. The danger of such a view of the curriculum, as Tattum and Tattum (1992) argue, is that: 'Cross-curricular work in personal and social education will be lost if teachers retreat into subject specialisms.'

Each teacher, then, must look to the *affective* aspects of curriculum delivery and not only the *cognitive*. The National Curriculum Council points out in Circular No. 6 (1989) that the affective curriculum 'cannot be left to chance but needs to be co-ordinated as an explicit part of a school's curriculum policy, both inside and outside the formal timetable'. Materials need to take account of the pupils' age and rate of development.

Rigby and Slee in Australia (1991) suggest that the older pupils become the less likely they are to sympathise with the victim. They found that:

> the majority of children were opposed to bullying and tended to be supportive of victims. However, the trend towards diminishing sympathy for the victim with increasing age, a trend evident for each sex, implies that that majority gradually erodes the longer children stay at school.

This has implications for the timing of interventions and for the nature of the curriculum materials themselves, for clearly these materials must be developmental if they are to have any impact. The earlier children encounter anti-bullying materials, the more effective will they be. This suggests that materials aimed at pupils at transfer are likely to be the most effective in countering bullying in any school.

This book confirms what many teachers already implicitly understand: low self-esteem is both cause and effect of bullying; many pupils bully others to improve their self-esteem; cooperative behaviour in a supportive atmosphere is likely to enhance children's self-esteem (Rigby and Slee, 1989).

Materials which actively encourage co-operative group work are more likely to be effective than those requiring pupils to work in isolation. Although further research is needed in these areas, the curriculum initiatives here described reinforce this view.

A variety of approaches have been described for introducing a behaviour policy into the school. These approaches have elements in common and can be considered as a series of steps.

- *Step one:* decide who should be involved in drawing up the policy. As staff at Glapton discovered, it is sometimes difficult to work to an agenda partially set by others — governors, ancillary staff, parents, pupils. Yet if schools are to recruit the support of these people, they too must have some input into the policy so they feel some sense of ownership.

- *Step two:* define what the policy should contain. This needs to be a whole-school exercise. At first, many schools come up with what pupils should *not* do; the policy is presented as a series of negatives. As the Elton Report (1989) points out, this must be avoided, by considering from the outset what is wanted of the pupils. The processes adopted by the staff at schools in the management section of this book illustrate what might happen.

- *Step three:* produce a document in the form of a set of procedures. Determining these procedures clarifies what actions should be taken in certain situations. Policies written as a series of aims may, despite the best intentions, do little more than gather dust, unless it is clear how these aims are to be achieved. And what governors, ancillary staff, pupils, parents, the school Psychological Service and the school Welfare Service should do to contribute.

- *Step four:* devise methods of monitoring, review and evaluation — perhaps the most important and most difficult task. Effective performance indicators must be provided if the policy is to have any credibility.

- *Step five:* Finally, all this must be communicated to pupils and their parents and to all those working in the school, so that it is fully understood. This book has outlined some ways to achieve this. A pupil code of conduct, written by the pupils for the pupils, is an effective form of communication. A series of assemblies on the topic of bullying, delivered by staff or pupils, is another way for the school

SPHERES OF INVOLVEMENT

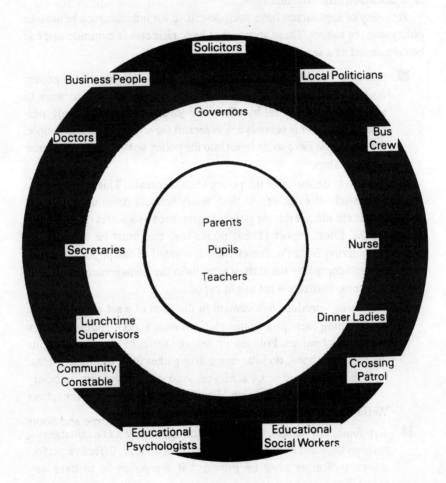

to make its intentions clear. So are videos made by pupils or professionals. Noticeboards can be used to inform not only pupils but also other visitors to the school. Newsletters can provide information in an accessible manner. Local newspapers have also been fruitfully involved, as at Lakeside School where a reporter and photographer made the most of pupils' attempts to raise the issue.

The long term responses include informing the entire community of the school's intentions and advising how they can play their part. Tattum and Tattum (1992) present a useful model of how a wide range of people can be incorporated into the tackling of bullying (See Spheres of Involvement, Page 186).

To present the school's efforts at tackling the problem to the wider community requires sensitivity to the community's perceptions. Many schools have noted their concern that the communities they serve might misinterpret their aims. Tackling bullying in a concerted way can be misunderstood as indicating that 'we have a problem' and this must be avoided. It can be attempted only when the school is satisfied with the interaction between teachers, pupils and their parents and with the involvement in the anti-bullying programme of the other adults who participate in the everyday life of a school; secretaries, lunchtime supervisors, nurses and so on, as happened so successfully at Millfield. Those with professional interest in adopting a more pro-active approach to the problems caused by serious bullying, like Educational Welfare Officers or Educational Psychologists, must also be given confidence that the school is achieving its aims. These can be professional catalysts for a great deal of good work, as we saw at Beaumont Leys School. Having achieved this, schools can reach out beyond the school boundaries and the direct influence of the school.

Local industrialists can be approached to sponsor initiatives in, say, a playground project. The community constable can be advised of the school's intentions and the policy implemented out of school hours and at weekends. Local schools can form clusters, in a concerted attempt to combat bullying throughout the community, as has happened at both Minsthorpe and South Craven. The School and Community Model summarises such an approach (page 188).

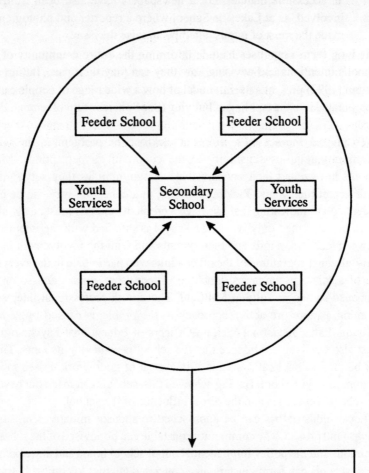

The School and Community Approach

Feeder School

Feeder School

Youth Services

Secondary School

Youth Services

Feeder School

Feeder School

School Liaison:
Police, Outside Agencies

4. Summary

If children are to learn in an atmosphere free from humiliation, abuse and oppression, schools must move from inconsistent and piecemeal reactions to separate incidents of bullying, towards developing a consistent set of procedures which everyone in the school knows, understands and trusts. This alone will create a more positive ethos in the school. Good practice can be disseminated, adopted, built upon. By canvassing the views of everyone involved in school, including pupils, a sense of 'ownership' can be fostered as the policy is implemented and schools can positively influence the communities which they serve.

The ways of working outlined in this book present a challenge to schools. It is a challenge worth rising to, as the schools here testify, for it can benefit all our children.

References

ACE (1990) Governors and Bullying. Bulletin 34. London: ACE

Ahmad, Y. and Smith, P.K. (1990) 'Behavioural measures: bullying in schools'. Newsletter of Association for Child Psychology and Psychiatry, 12, pp.44-47

Askew, S. (1988) 'Aggressive Behaviour in Boys: to what extent is it institutionalised?' In D. Tattum and D. Lane (ed.) Bullying in Schools. Stoke-on-Trent: Trentham Books

Besag, V. (1989) Bullies and Victims in Schools. Milton Keynes: Open University Press

Blatchford, P. (1989) Playtime in the Primary School. Problems and Improvements. Windsor: NFER-Nelson

DES (1987) Education Observed 5. Good behaviour and discipline in schools. Stanmore, Middlesex: DES Publications

DFE (1992) Framework for the Inspection of Schools. Paper for Consultation. London: DFE Publications

Elliott, M. (1991) Bullying: A Practical Guide to Coping for Schools. Harlow: Longman

Elton report (1989) Discipline in Schools. London: HMSO

Eron, L.D., Huesmann, L.R., Dubow, E., Romanoff, R. and Yarmel, P.W. (1987) 'Aggression and its correlates over 22 years'. In D. Crowell, I. Evans and C. O'Donnell (eds.) Childhood Aggression and Violence. New York: Plenum Press

Herbert, G. (1988) 'A whole-curriculum approach to bullying'. In D. Tattum and D. Lane (eds.) Bullying in Schools. Stoke-on-Trent: Trentham Books

Kelly, E. and Cohn, T. (1988) Racism in Schools — New Research Evidence. Stoke-on-Trent: Trentham Books

La Fontaine, J. (1991) Bullying: a Child's View. London: Calouste Gulbenkian Foundation

La Fontaine, J. and Morris, S. (1992) The Boarding School Line. January-July 1991. London: ChildLine

Macdonald, I., Bhavnani, R., Kahn, L. and John, G. (1989) Murder in the Playground. The Report of the MacDonald Inquiry into Racism and Racist Violence in Manchester Schools. London: Longsight Press

Marland, M. (1989) The Tutor and The Tutor Group. Harlow: Longman

Mellor, A. (1990) 'Bullying in Scottish secondary schools'. Spotlights, No. 23, Scottish Council for Research in Education.

Newson, J. and Newson, E. (1984) Parents' Perspectives on Children's Behaviour in School. In N. Frude and G. Gault (eds.) Disruptive Behaviour in Schools. Chichester: Wiley

Olweus, D. (1978) Aggression in the Schools: Bullies and Whipping Boys. Washington DC: Wiley

Olweus, D. (1989) Bully/victim problems among school children: basic facts and effects of a School Based Intervention Program'. In K. Rubin and D. Peplar (eds.) The Development and Treatment of Children's Aggression. New Jersey: Erlbaum

O'Moore, A.M. and Hillery, B. (1991) 'What do teachers need to know?' In M. Elliott (ed.) Bullying: A Practical Guide to Coping for Schools. Harlow, Longman

Reid, K. (1988) 'Bullying and Persistent School Absenteeism'. In D. Tattum and D. Lane (eds) Bullying in Schools. Stoke-on-Trent: Trentham Books.

Rigby, K. and Slee, P.T. (1990) 'Victims and bullies in school communities'. Journal of the Australian Society of Victimology, 1, (2), pp.23-8

Rigby, K. and Slee, P.T. (1991) 'Bullying among Australian school children: Reported behaviour and attitudes to victims'. Journal of Social Psychology, 131, pp.615-29

Roland, E. (1988) 'Bullying: The Scandinavian Research Tradition'. In D. Tattum and D. Lane (eds.) Bullying in Schools. Stoke-on-Trent: Trentham Books

Stephenson, P. and Smith, D. (1988) 'Bullying in the Junior School'. In D. Tattum and D. Lane (eds.) Bullying in Schools. Stoke-on-Trent: Trentham Books

Tattum, D.P. (ed.) (1993) Understanding and Managing Bullying. Oxford: Heinemann

Tattum, D.P. and Lane, D.A. (eds.) (1988) Bullying in Schools. Stoke-on-Trent: Trentham Books

Tattum, D.P. and Herbert, G. (1990) Bullying: A Positive Response. Advice for Parents, Governors and Staff in Schools. Cardiff: Cardiff Institute of Higher Education

Tattum, D.P. and Tattum, E. (1992) Social Education and Personal Development. London: David Fulton Publications

Tattum, D.P. and Tattum, E. (1992) 'Bullying: A Whole-school response'. In N. Jones and E. Baglin-Jones (eds) Learning to Behave. London: Kogan Page

Yates, C. and Smith, R.K. (1989) 'Bullying in two English Comprehensives'. In E. Roland and E. Munthe (eds) Bullying: An International Perspective. London: David Fulton Publications

Ziegler, S. and Rosenstein-Manner, M. (1991) Bullying at School: Toronto in an International Context (No. 196R), Research Services. Toronto: Board of Education

Author Index

ACE, 10
Ahmad, Y. and Smith, P.K., 8
Askew, S., 62
Besag, V., 47
Blatchford, P., 7
DES, 163
DFE, 4
Elliott, M., 34
Elton Report, 3, 5, 19, 43, 52, 146, 185
Eron, L.D., 9
Herbert, G., 62
Kelly, E. and Cohn, T., 7
La Fontaine, J., 2, 3, 62, 69, 180
La Fontaine, J. and Morris, S., 3, 115, 118
Macdonald, I. et al., 7
Marland, M., 78
Mellor, A., 8
Newson, J. and Newson, E., 7
Olweus, D., 8, 9, 12
O'Moore, A.M. and Hillery, B., 5
Reid, K., 126
Rigby, K. and Slee, P.T., 4, 8, 184

Roland, E., 13, 98
Roland,a E. and Munthe, E., 6
Stephenson, P. and Smith, D., 11, 98
Tattum, D.P., 6
Tattum, D.P. and Herbert, G., 1, 3, 13, 182
Tattum, D.P. and Tattum, E., 5, 10, 80, 86, 184, 187
Yates, C. and Smith, P.K., 8
Zeigler, S. and Rosenstein-Manner, M., 8

Subject Index

Adviser 109, 124, 146, 147
agencies — education and others
123-60
ancillary staff 24, 113
ABC (Anti-Bullying Campaign)
123-60
anti-bullying approaches 2
policies 33, 105, 108-11,
133-4, 136, 169, 171
programmes (also
campaigns) 2, 3, 63-4, 79, 147,
181
strategies 32
assemblies 91-4, 139
Australia 8

Big Brun Theatre Company 63
behaviour policy 19-28, 184-7
modification 17
boarders 86
Boarding School Line 3, 115-16,
117
Bully Free Zone 174

bullying
definitions 6
dealing with 107, 110
extent of 7, 9
fact or fiction 90
long-term effects 9-10
nature of 6-7, 70-2, 117,
132-4, 141-2, 158-9
plan of action 99
whole school approach
10-13, 29
Bullying Line 127, 131

Calouste Gulbenkian Foundation
(see Gulbenkian Foundation)
chaplain 42, 75, 112, 142
ChildLine 2, 91, 116, 117
Children Act 46, 75, 113
Children's Charter 11, 162, 173-7
citizenship 80, 83
classroom expectations 102
Cleveland 8
cluster approach (also policy) 59,
96-103, 187

code of secrecy 11
community 104, 108-11
    ethos 113
    policy 173, 175
conference, for pupils 151-160
Council of Europe 2
counsellor 112
Crime Prevention Panel 173, 175, 176
crisis-management 11
cross-curricular themes 80-4
curriculum 2, 13, 45, 48, 61-84, 88-91, 96, 164, 184,
    affective 68, 80, 83, 184
    cognitive 80, 83, 184

Dormitories 43
drama 64, 67, 76, 95, 151

Education Reform Act 45, 163
Education Support Service 145
Education Welfare Officer 18, 123, 126, 139, 165, 169, 171, 172, 185, 187
Education Psychologist 24, 37, 103, 106, 111, 123, 146, 165, 169, 172, 187,   185
English 82-4, 89-91
Equal Opportunities 16, 24, 49, 103, 108
Governing Body, 10, 52, 67, 146
governors 24, 34, 52, 108, 136, 147
Gulbenkian Foundation 1, 2, 3, 42, 123, 161
Gwynedd Education Authority 163-72

Heads of Year 114
Houseparents 112-14
House prefects 115, 118

staff (also master/mistress) 41-2, 47, 72, 112
    structure 44
HMC 45
HMI 163, 164

Independent Schools 41-7, 69-75, 112-22
initiation ceremonies 85-6, 116
INSET 22, 30, 37, 46, 48, 49, 96, 111, 145, 146, 179

Life Skills 76
Local Education Authorities 16, 17, 19, 106, 161-178
Lothian Regional Council 11, 173-8
Lunchtime Organisers (also Mid-day Supervisors) 53-60, 180

Management 2, 15-60, 61-2
    tasks 18
    team 49, 126

National Curriculum (see also curriculum) 36, 49, 61-2, 80, 163, 170
Neti-Neti Theatre Company 139
North Manchester District Support Team 58
Norway 2, 7, 8, 9, 98
nurse 67

parents 26, 67, 71, 109, 136, 147, 177
parents' newsletter 140
persistent absentees 126
Personal and Social Education (also pastoral care) 15, 19, 22, 24, 30, 34, 42,   44-6, 49, 64, 76, 77, 89, 98, 108, 113, 114, 134, 139-40, 143, 181

playground (also playtime) 7, 16,
    24-5, 37-8, 53-60, 146, 187
police 109, 187, 162, 173, 175
policy statement 12
praise 57-8
PTA 176
Punch and Judy 67
Pyramid system 104-11

Quaker Peace Education Project
    124, 151-60
questionnaire (see also survey) 43,
    69-70, 93-5, 9708, 119-22, 139,
    144, 165-8, 182

racial harassment 3, 7, 17, 136
Record of Achievement 83,
147-50, 181
Religious Education 77, 145
rules 47

Safer Schools, Safer Cities Project
    106
sanctions 56
School and Community approach
    186
School Development Plan 134
School Medical Officer 114
self-esteem (also self-image) 5,
    10, 29-30, 46, 48
sexual harassment 7, 17
sixth formers 45, 73
Special Needs 103, 135
Sphere of Involvement 186
stereotyping 94
Student Council 135
survey (see also questionnaires)
    132, 137-8

Teacher Effectiveness Training 30
themes 2
transition (also transfer) 2, 85-122
Travelling Roadshow 173-5

United Kingdom 2, 4, 181
University of Ulster 151

Welsh Office 164

Youth Service 109